ASTRID WAGNER

THE
ABYSSES
OF JOSEF F

Imprint

First edition, May 2023

ISBN: 9798393028695

Author and copyright: 2023, Dr Astrid Wagner

Website: www.anwalt-wagner.at

Translated by: Monika Schulz, BA MA MA
A professional freelance translator and certified court interpreter living and working in Vienna.

Portrait photo: Dr Astrid Wagner: © Marcus Elöd Deak

Cover photo: © Helmut Fohringer/APA

www.picturedesk.com

Illustrations: Wolfgang Tillich, born on 21 November 1964. Freelance architect and artist working in his studio in Kremstal.

All rights reserved.

Preface

This book is about a true crime. It sheds light on the processes inside the perpetrator. Processes that could provide instructive insights into the causes of human aberrations, up to and including the most serious crimes. And it gives food for thought, on questions like: Are criminals born or made? What role does early childhood play? How should we deal with mentally ill offenders? Can they be treated effectively?

I can only imagine the suffering caused by the actions of Josef F. Nevertheless, I have left out the perspective of the victims and relatives. Those who take offense to this should not read this book. It is a deliberate omission, because it was important to me to protect these people and their private spheres of life.

For the same reasons, I have refrained from describing the crimes committed by Josef F. As far as any similarities with victims or relatives arise, all events and circumstances presented in this book are fictionalised. The illustrations derive from the imagination of the artist Wolfgang Tillich and have no relation to real events or places.

In my law office in July 2022

The letter filed by my secretary in my usual court mail immediately catches my eye. It is written with an old mechanical typewriter, and the envelope is handwritten. Judging by the somewhat shaky, yet assertive handwriting, it is probably an elderly gentleman. As indicated by the sender's address, he is in the largest men's prison in Austria, in Stein an der Donau.

A quick glance at my wristwatch shows almost 2 p.m., the first client will be arriving soon. I quickly open the envelope and begin to read.

"I, Josef F, have written a manuscript about my life. I would like to publish it as a book. I am reaching out to you with the question or rather request whether you could support me in this endeavour. It particularly describes the events that led to my arrest and conviction. I have..."

"Ding-dong". The intercom on my desk sounds, and I pick up. "Yes, please?" My voice sounds impatient, which I immediately regret. The hectic nature of the legal profession means constantly being pulled out of activities you have started, reacting at lightning speed, and always staying flexible. I have long since become accustomed to this, just as my employees have become accustomed to my occasionally quick-tempered reactions resulting thereof.

"Mr Maier is already here," my secretary and office manager Silvia informs me, slightly intimidated.

"I'll be ready in a moment," I tell her and quickly scan the remaining lines of the letter. All at once I realise who has written to me.

Almost fifteen years ago, a criminal case uncovered in Austria had put the small country in the spotlight of the entire world. A successful entrepreneur from the Austrian district capital of Amstetten had to stand trial before a jury for the crimes of murder, multiple rapes, slave trade, deprivation of liberty, aggravated coercion, and incest. Inconceivable crimes that prompted the court to commission the renowned psychiatric expert Dr Adelheid Kastner to assess the defendant. She diagnosed him with a "severe combined personality disorder and a disorder of sexual preference". Childhood experiences and a relationship with his mother characterised by extraordinarily coldness had led to "emotional invalidity". The expert even spoke of an "emotional illiterate", who had expressed sentences during the examination such as: "I lasted a long time for someone born to rape" and "there is an evil streak lurking in me".

Despite this "mental abnormality of a higher degree", as such severe personality disorders are referred to by the legislature, he was, however, fully legally responsible. The defendant himself pleaded fully guilty: "I regret from the bottom of my heart what I have done to my family. Unfortunately, I cannot make it up to them anymore." The unanimously reached guilty verdict by the jury resulted in a life sentence for Josef F, along with a commitment to an institution for mentally abnormal offenders.

"I accept the verdict," the defendant declared in a firm voice after the verdict was pronounced. He did not even want to listen to the legal instruction of the presiding judge.

It was a crime that, due to its uniqueness, had not only captivated the justice system, but also drawn reporter teams from all over the world to swarm the small district capital and its courthouse with their satellite dishes. A renowned French writer dedicated a literary work to the outrageous events[1], and the Austrian punk rock scene was inspired to create a music album[2]. To this day, countless documentaries and films circulate on the internet, including an apparently illegally recorded audio tape made in prison.

A few years ago, he changed his surname. According to the official explanation, his former name should not stand in his way in case of his release. In this publication, I use the initial letter of his old name, which is inextricably linked to his story.

Is Josef F really an "emotional illiterate"? I want to get an impression of him myself.

---

[1] *Régis Jauffret: "Claustria", Paris 2012*
[2] *"Land der Keller" [Land of the Cellars], 2019*

Stein Prison, interrogation zone, in July 2022

About a week after receiving the letter, I enter the interrogation zone of the prison. "He's in room 3," the officer tells me kindly.

The tiny meeting rooms intended for lawyers and officials are separated only by thin wooden walls. The furnishings are sparse, with orange tabletops and light grey walls adorned with a large, red-bordered sign displaying a camera warning: "This room is video-monitored".

"Hello, I'm Doctor Wagner," I introduce myself. Josef F is now eighty-seven years old and looks naturally older than he did in the newspaper photos. But his blue-grey eyes sparkle at the sight of me, and he smiles warmly and shakes my hand. I sense energy. Willpower. Determination. No trace of dementia, as the media had repeatedly rumoured in recent years. No, this man here is by no means a helpless old man.

And he immediately flatters me. "I thought of you many times. I read your book about Jack Unterweger. It impressed me how you stood by him. That's why I wanted to meet you. At last, I gave myself a jolt and wrote to you."

I can't help but smile. The conversation is casual, almost pleasant. That may seem strange given his crimes. But the profession of being a criminal defence lawyer has become too ingrained in me. I have always tried to get to the bottom of so-called evil, to look into the abysses, to explore the causes of crime. If you want to trace the roots of evil, you have to meet your counterpart on an equal footing. Not to judge and condemn, but to listen…

Even at this first encounter, I learn a detail from this person's childhood that makes me think. However, he does not complain about it or seek sympathy. Rather, he tells it quite dryly, as if he were still searching for his own abysses. As a young child, his mother always tied him to a table when she went to work. Just so that the boy wouldn't do any mischief... He spent hours like that in solitary confinement. A plate with food lay in front of him like a dog's food bowl.

No, he doesn't hate his mother at all. Those had just been difficult times. War and poverty had shaped her.

.

In my law office in July 2022

One week later. I have been in court until late afternoon, now I still had to handle the mail and prepare the files for tomorrow.

A thick envelope made of brown wrapping paper, with several stamps and the note "personal" written on it, was lying on my desk. I tear it open impatiently and a bundle of thin, closely printed sheets of paper tumbles out. The manuscript. It is quite extensive, a whole two hundred and twenty-six pages. As I curiously flip through it, I decide to have my secretary Silvia type it out before I start editing. A tedious undertaking, but unavoidable. Josef F owns a small PC, but it is strictly forbidden to take any electronic storage device out of the prison.

Silvia is excited about my new project and immediately gets started. She is still young and idealistic and has always wanted to work in a law firm specialising in criminal law. But this job comes with many challenges. One must endure difficult clients, develop a thick skin, yet at the same time try not to lose faith in the good in people.

Silvia is my first critic. The typing drags on for a few weeks, and she keeps sending me her impressions via WhatsApp: "Page by page, I believe I am penetrating deeper and deeper into this person's inner being. It's very interesting for me to learn about his view of things, even though I can't comprehend everything, and some of it makes my hair stand on end. Has he even understood the impact of his actions? In any case, there must have been deep emotional wounds that led this person to develop in such a way".

"Deep emotional wounds." Evidently, Silvia has already learned a lot during the two years she has been working for me. No one is born a criminal. There is always a story behind a crime.

And it is precisely this story that I want to pursue in the case of Josef F. In the following months, I will pay him several visits in prison in order to gain insights into his soul. However, I could only partially comply with his wish to publish his manuscript. For reasons of media law, it is not allowed to report on the course of events and details of the crimes he committed, as the privacy of the persons involved could be affected. Be that as it may, the crimes committed by Josef F have been widely reported in the media. What interests me is something completely different: it is what is going on in his head. How he thinks. What drove him to commit these acts and how he processed them.

***

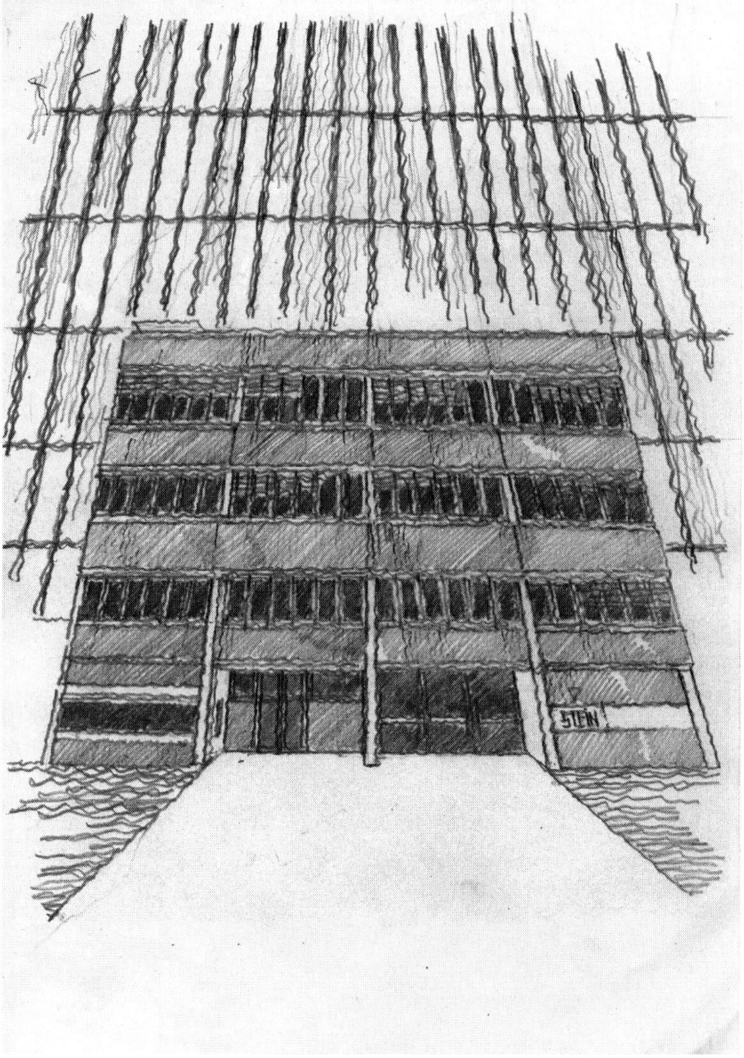
STEIN

Editing the original manuscript proved to be a tedious task, especially when it came to the strict censorship imposed by media law. Any descriptions that could touch on the lives of the victims or their relatives had to be excluded for legal reasons. Ultimately, the present work has gained expressive power through this strict reduction to its core theme. What remains of the original two hundred and twenty-six pages written in narrow lines by Josef F, are fragmentary descriptions, stripped of superfluous details. Dry in style, bland in expression, yet outrageous in view of the reality of the events in which they are embedded. In this way, they become a parable of what constitutes their author. An outwardly dry, socially adapted person, who inwardly, however, was apparently driven by inconceivable constraints, not to say, even tormented by demons.

I embarked on a search of the abysses in this person. Over many months, I had long conversations with him, which I have reproduced in the present work with his consent. The moods and situations in which I experienced Josef F were diverse. He seemed thoughtful, sad, worried, then again mischievous and funny. I largely refrained from making a judgement. I would rather leave it to the readers to ask themselves questions such as: How could the successful businessman Josef F lead a double life over decades? Did everyone, including the authorities, look the other way? Is Josef F emotionally illiterate? How much of him is in ourselves? Don't we all have our dark side, our personal abysses, our very own cellar where we hide our forbidden longings and desires from the outside world?

"Mentally abnormal": The psychiatric detention

When reading this book, you should always keep one thing in mind: It is the subjective perception of a person who was legally classified as a "mentally abnormal offender" by a court due to his actions.

But what does "mentally abnormal" mean in Austrian criminal law? Its legal basis is regulated in § 21 of the Austrian Criminal Code. The court committed Josef F to an "institution for mentally abnormal lawbreakers". Of course, this was not a punishment, but a so-called measure: The court orders this in addition to the sentenced penalty, if a serious crime has been committed under the influence of - according to the definition at the time - a "mental or psychic abnormality of a higher degree", with a psychiatric prognosis report affirming the dangerousness of the convicted person. Such "abnormalities" include serious mental illnesses, such as delusional disorders or severe personality disorders. If the mental illness is so severe that the person concerned cannot be held criminally responsible for his or her actions, he or she is placed in the institution without a sentence being imposed.

It was different with Josef F. The court-appointed psychiatric expert, Dr Adelheid Kastner, had diagnosed him with a severe combined personality disorder, but his "capacity for control" was still intact. Thus, Josef F was classified as sane and held responsible for his actions. In addition to the life sentence, the court ordered him to be placed in an institution for mentally abnormal offenders.

The so-called "forensic detention" was once proposed by the great judicial reformer Christian Broda[3], as an opportunity and therapy for mentally ill offenders. Over the decades, however, it has degenerated into a detention centre for those who were no longer wanted in society. In practice, mentally ill offenders are still mainly housed in conventional prisons, as the currently existing special forensic facilities in Göllersdorf and Asten (which only opened as a forensic prison in 2010) do not have sufficient capacity. Josef F was also sent to the Stein Prison after his conviction, admittedly in the unit intended for "mentally disordered lawbreakers". Each new Minister of Justice promised a major reform of the psychiatric detention upon taking office. Expert committees were appointed, but before anything concrete was established, his term of office had already ended due to political conflicts.

Meanwhile, the number of those institutionalised rose steadily from year to year. In December 2022, the Minister of Justice finally implemented the reform proposal that had been lying in the drawer for years. The noble goal was to bring the psychiatric detention closer to its original purpose of "therapy instead of punishment". Whether this will succeed is doubtful, especially since the important issue of uniform standardisation of psychiatric assessments was left out. Instead, the admission requirements were somewhat tightened. Now the underlying offence must be punishable with a term of imprisonment of more than three years, unless a psychiatric prognosis concludes that the person concerned may commit serious offences against life and limb, or sexual offences in the future. The judiciary thus

---

[3] *Austrian Minister of Justice from 1960 to 1966 and 1970 to 1983*

places the responsibility in the hands of psychiatric experts, for whom, however, uniform standards are still lacking. It is therefore a reform that is likely to come at the expense of legal certainty. Instead, it brought cosmetic changes to the terminology. The term "mental or psychological abnormality of a higher degree" was replaced by the possibly less stigmatising formulation "serious and persistent mental disorder". Instead of "placement in an institution for mentally abnormal offenders", "placement in a forensic therapy centre" is being used now. It was also announced that such centres will be increasingly established and expanded in the future.

The reform is unlikely to put an end to the misery of the psychiatric detention. Not least because of the lack of resources for adequate treatment. Much seems to fail because of money, sometimes also because of the lack of will. Mentally ill offenders are a marginal issue that does not win votes.

In my law office in July 2022

It has become late, the last client has just left the office. I fetch the typed manuscript from the desk drawer, squeeze a small espresso from the coffee machine and take a seat in my large winged armchair - a sixties-style piece covered in large pop art motifs that I acquired in a workshop for people with disabilities. The shade of the large antique floor lamp with colourful fringes creates a pleasant, warm light. I begin to read.

Josef F: A clarification up front

I, Josef F, was sentenced to life imprisonment by an Austrian jury court almost fifteen years ago for murder, rape, deprivation of liberty, aggravated coercion and incest. I had pleaded guilty and accepted the sentence immediately.

During the long years of imprisonment, I wrote down my life story. The descriptions of sexual adventures come from my imagination. Although they are inspired by true events, they are been altered to such an extent that any similarities with living or already deceased persons are purely coincidental and in no way intended. Rather, they are dreams and mental journeys that make my everyday life in prison bearable.

***

Looking back, I blame myself that it had to come to this. I had been working successfully for decades as a general agent for a Danish concrete pipe construction company. My territory covered the whole of Austria, where I had to look after about eighty companies and was therefore on the road accordingly often. During the summer season, I also ran a large hotel with a restaurant, bar and attached camping site at Lake Mondsee. With all these obligations and tasks, there was little time left for the family. Far too little! I increasingly got the feeling that something was threatening to slip away from me.

Suddenly, it was there. The thought. As if out of nowhere, like an impulse that flashed in my mind. Wandering aimlessly in it. Like a small, lost leaf swirling over the asphalt of the road before being carried away by the wind. A vague idea I was playing with. Yes, at first it was just a mind game. But I got used to it. The thought that had seemed so absurd, so outrageous before, took on shape. It became a fixed idea that gradually took root in my mind. I had always been a person who made decisions alone. One day, I knew what I had to do. My mind was made up. All that remained was to wait for the right opportunity.

On that rainy Saturday morning, the time had come. The thought had turned into reality.

The next morning, I filed a missing person's report with the local gendarmerie. The officer carefully recorded everything and explained, "She is over eighteen and can do whatever she wants."

***

No one was allowed to know what it felt like on the inside. It was not easy. The thoughts of what I had done were constantly circling inside me. I was constantly under pressure. There was no one I could confide in. I had to look ahead and pursue the path I had taken.

In my law office in July 2022

"A solitary decision". I put the pages aside. I am a little stirred up inside and have to let the things I have just read sink in. I put another capsule into the coffee machine, press the button and wait until the small cup is filled with the aromatic, hot drink. Then I take a strong sip, and go back to work. While stirring the remaining creamy foam, all kinds of thoughts run through my head. What goes on in a person's mind when he talks up his crime in such a... yes, euphemistic way! What did he tell me on my first visit? No, what he had done was not right. That's why he had accepted the sentence immediately. But his words read very differently. I know this from many criminal trials. What happened is being suppressed, blocked out, even denied. But Josef F at least seems to suspect how things are with him. "I am a torn person, with passions that I cannot control," he had told the psychiatric expert Dr Kastner during the examination.

Stein Prison, visitor room, in August 2022

I never minded spending a little waiting time in the visitor room at Stein Prison, because it is attractively designed. There are pictures and hand-painted clocks on the walls, with handicrafts and pottery in a corner. The works of art were created by inmates as part of occupational therapy. Particularly appealing is a large loom, whose red-white-red painted frame is interwoven with cords of different thicknesses in bold colours. It was designed by the artist Johann Peter Preiss, who was sentenced to life imprisonment, and is meant to show the flow of life. The colours stand for the different stages of life, the thickened knots for strokes of fate or unexpected turns. In between, there are paving stones attached to the cords with wires, symbolising the time of imprisonment in the Stein Prison.

Since the outbreak of the Corona pandemic, visits have to be booked in advance by telephone, which means there is hardly any waiting time. It's a pity, really, because the brief moments of contemplation while looking at the small works of art did me good.

When I am called to the interrogation area, Josef F is usually already waiting for me. He does not have too far to go from his solitary cell, where he has been housed for many years. Solitary confinement is not unusual for those sentenced to long prison terms. The situation is different with pre-trial detention. As a rule, this is not spent in a penal institution, but in one of the provincial court prisons, and these are usually hopelessly overcrowded. In the Vienna-Josefstadt Prison, for example, the cells intended for two people are usually occupied by four or even more inmates. After the judgement becomes final, the pre-trial detention is converted into penal detention with full credit for the already served pre-trial detention. It then takes a few more weeks, sometimes even months, until the so-called classification: The Federal Ministry of Justice decides in which prison the sentence shall be served, taking into account the type of sentence imposed and the personality of the convicted person. Of course, in view of resocialisation, the social and family situation of the inmate is also considered. The place of residence of the relatives is taken into account in order to facilitate the visiting possibilities as much as possible. Convicts with no criminal record are detained in the prison for first-time offenders. This goes hand in hand with some forms of relief, such as a residential sub-unit, where the cell doors remain open during the day in a living area with its own kitchen, the sanitary facilities and a washing machine. They are only locked up around 9 p.m., until 7 a.m.

Even if the social romantic notions of a "prison-free society" of Christian Broda[4] are long gone, and a more restrictive zeitgeist has taken hold in prisons in the meantime, and many ideas and projects simply fail due to lack of funding, it is still true that maintaining positive social and family contacts is crucial to prevent recidivism. Initially, the inmate only receives "glass visitations" - a thick pane of glass separates him from the visitors, and communication takes place via a telephone.

With good behaviour, he is soon granted a table visit, where he is allowed to sit at a table with his visitors, admittedly guarded by prison guards. If there are no security concerns, the inmate is eventually entitled to a long-term visit, popularly known as a "cuddle cell". These are specially equipped small flats within the prison, where the inmate may spend a few hours undisturbed and without surveillance with close persons.

---

[4] *Austrian Minister of Justice from 1960 to 1966 and 1970 to 1983. During his term of office, Austrian criminal law was fundamentally reformed.*

Since he had no prior criminal record, Josef F was classified as a first-time offender. In his case, however, there was the special measure of the psychiatric detention. Inmates on whom such a measure was imposed due to their mental and emotional abnormality in addition to serving their sentence, are accommodated in special sections of the prison. Their daily routine differs in that they are expected to work on processing their crime in psychiatric and psychotherapeutic therapy sessions. Otherwise, however, they are "completely normal" inmates who also have to work in prison. Stein Prison has its own workshops and businesses. The printing press deserves special mention. It supplies the entire Austrian judiciary system with printed materials. Being able to work is of fundamental importance to prisoners. It gives structure and meaning to their day. Although the income is minimal, it is enough to satisfy modest needs such as additional purchases for food, stationery or smoking, telephone calls with relatives or lawyers. Unfortunately, telephone charges are higher than on the free market. Contrary to popular belief, prison inmates also have to pay for electricity. There is a charge per device, and for example, Stein Prison currently has a cap of thirty-five euros per cell.

***

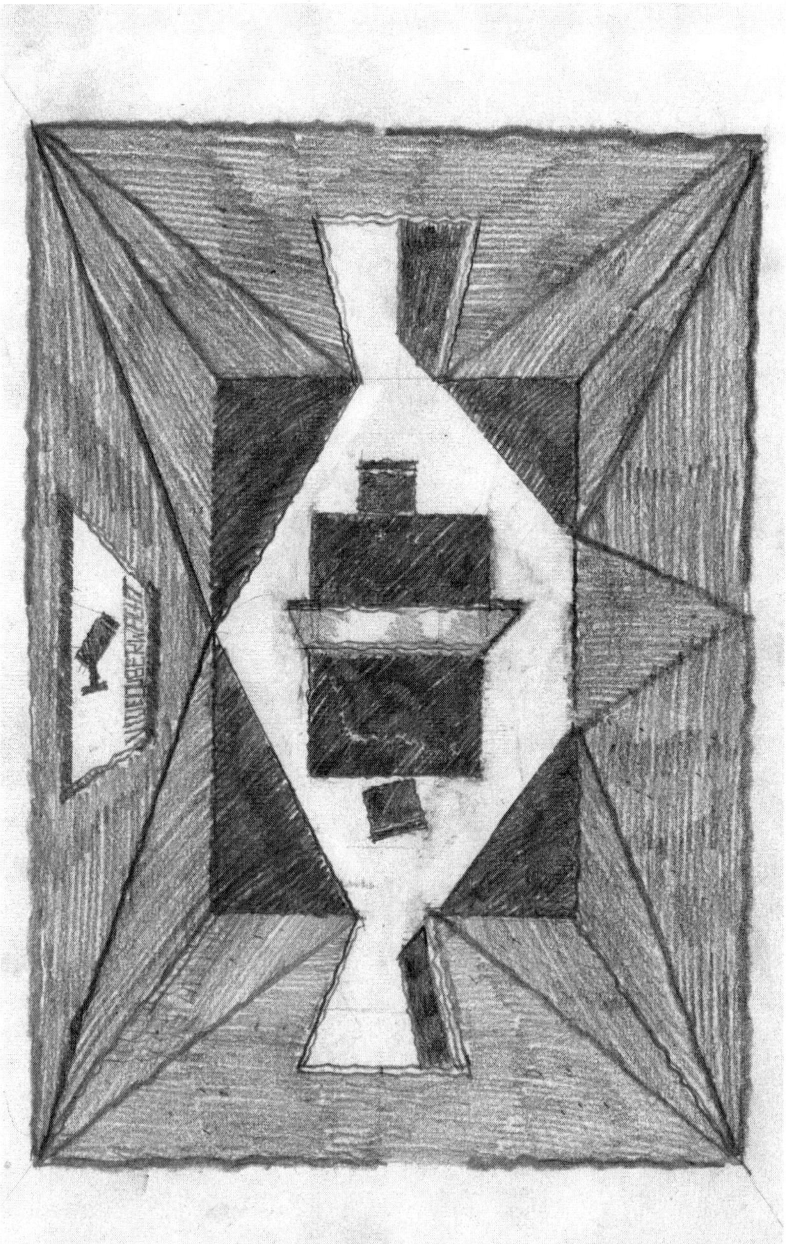

Josef F seems a little tired today. His grey eyes look at me dully, yet he tries a polite smile. Spontaneously, I decide to cheer him up with a question he will probably be happy to answer.

"What are you proud of in your life?"

Indeed, he doesn't have to think twice. "Of my professional achievements and successes. I have always been one who tackles things. In Ghana, for example. The company I worked for was a subcontractor of a large electrical corporation and was building shortwave transmitters. They urgently needed technicians, but everyone was scared as shit because there was this terrible disease raging there at the time, what was its name... ah, Ebola! However, I was young, foolish, and above all, curious about the world. The contract was initially limited to a year, but afterwards automatically extended. My family didn't come with me, I thought it was too dangerous for them at the time. I met this great woman in Ghana. An artist from a good family. She was very empathetic and showed me her beautiful country. I saw areas that you can't get to as a tourist. She was fifteen years older than me and unfortunately already passed away. With her, I have a son who has become something. A highly respectable person, he studied law and is professionally successful! I think if he were in Austria, he would surely be here for me."

In my law office in August 2022

Josef F is captivating me more and more, by now I am almost a little obsessed with his story. I have long since looked up his CV. Despite difficult starting conditions, he had a remarkable professional career. At the age of fifteen, after completing secondary school, he went to Linz without informing his mother and looked for an apprenticeship as an electrician. He then turned to the welfare services, which placed him in a church-run home. "I still can't explain how I found the courage to do that," he was to say to the psychiatric expert decades later. He completed his apprenticeship and journeyman's examination with honours and then worked as an electrician for a nationalised steel company in Linz. And he continued his education. In the evenings, he attended the school for master craftsmen and a preparatory course for the higher technical training institutes. In between, he earned good money away on assembly jobs in Luxembourg and Ghana, where he spent one and a half years. At the age of 34, he became the operations manager of a concrete company in his hometown. He quit after two years to take over the Austrian general agency of a large Danish concrete pipe construction company. In 1973, he also leased a hotel with an attached camping site at Lake Mondsee, which he expanded to three hundred seats and ran for twenty-three years. He was also successful as a landlord, acquiring several properties in Upper Austria. He worked as a general agent until his retirement at the age of sixty.

So that was his official life: the successful, smart, somewhat conservative entrepreneur from the countryside. But beneath this unremarkable surface, there must have been a great deal of turmoil. The psychiatric expert Dr Adelheid Kastner aptly formulated it with a symbolic image: *"He has much of a volcano. Beneath an inconspicuous, relatively un-differentiated, almost banal-looking, at any rate unspectacular surface that impresses with its unpretentious average appearance, lurks in an unfathomable depth that cannot be perceived from the outside, what he himself perceives about himself (even if only hinted at and undifferentiated), which he describes with the words that he (...) could also have done something worse, or when he explains that for someone born to rape, he had controlled himself a relatively long time."*

Josef F:

Chaotic images of undefinable monsters full of vengeful oaths had haunted me in confused dreams. I had woken up drenched in sweat and stared with open eyes into the darkness. It was pitch black and dead silent, as if no other being lived in this universe. All at once, the thought of what I had done entered my consciousness. A painful feeling of regret spread through me.

In my law office in August 2022

Once again, I took advantage of a free evening to read in the manuscript. Page after page, Josef F became more entangled in his crimes. Evil seemed to be slowly maturing inside him, unnoticed by others, hidden behind seemingly good intentions, as if he did not want to admit it himself. Until he commits the incomprehensible. I need a break and put the pages aside. But the thoughts of what I just read won't let me go. I have been dealing with criminals for decades and know that many of them lie to themselves. They develop their own theories and ideas that become immovably fixed in their brains. Probably, it is not possible for many of them to deal with their actions in any other way. They cannot bear the truth because they could not bear the guilt. This is especially the case with sexual offences. Disgust. Shame. Incest. If you want to understand the incomprehensible, you have to overcome the natural revulsion that acts like these trigger in us.

Josef F:

The business trip first took me through Upper Austria, where I had the most clients. I stayed there for a whole week.

I drove into town to have dinner. The waitress was an exceptionally pretty middle-aged woman, with whom I quickly struck up a conversation. When I said goodbye, she smiled promisingly and slipped me her room number. An opportunity I could not pass up. She welcomed me in a negligee, immediately grabbed me by the tie, pulled me into her room and stripped me of my clothes in a rush. Her desire was breath-taking, I quickly got going and pleased her in every way possible. When I put my clothes back on, she looked at me lasciviously and at the same time disappointed. "Are you already leaving?" As hard as it was to say goodbye to her, I had firmly resolved to go home that same night. "Come back soon," she whispered. I promised, even though I knew I would not be able to keep that promise.

I used to love being on the road, it was a welcomed distraction from home. Now, everything was different. I wanted to get my work appointments done quickly so that I could be back home as soon as possible. It was fear that drove me. The fear that it could be discovered: my secret.

Stein Prison, interrogation zone, in August 2022

"I am impressed by everything you have achieved in your life," I tell him. He smiles. "Many have envied my success. But they haven't seen the sacrifice behind it. The discipline, the hard work."

"What drove you, were you always ambitious?", I ask.

"Not really as a child. On the contrary, I often skipped school and hung around instead. I often felt lonely and somehow also rejected, yes, ignored."

"How did you get along with your classmates?"

"I was always polite, got along well with everyone. But I also didn't let anyone walk all over me. If I was attacked, I hit back. After all, I was a strong, athletic boy. School… Well, I got through primary school fairly badly. Then I went on to secondary school. There, too, I was a rather mediocre pupil. What I hated most was memorising poems. I still remember when I was asked by the class teacher, whose name was Sturm[5] by the way, to recite the poem 'The Bell'. I stood up in front of the whole class and said, 'I am the bell!' There was a roar of laughter! When I was once again hanging around the farmers instead of going to school, Mr Sturm suddenly came there. He was looking for me! I jumped up and ran away as if the storm was after me!"

"That was the case, after all," I interject with a grin, and he laughs. "Yes, exactly. But he didn't get me. I scrambled over a fence and hid in a potato field. There I heard him calling out, 'Why don't you come back to school? It would be a pity if you spoiled your future!' That sentence stuck in my mind. I felt so guilty and ashamed. That's when I resolved to pull myself together. It touched me how much this teacher cared for me. I didn't want to disappoint him anymore. I got better and better, especially in the technical subjects, because that was where my strengths lay. I wasn't so good in languages, I always just barely passed them. But then, in third grade, the English teacher, Reynolds was her name, gave me a B! I'm still moved today by how they looked after me to make something of me. The good grade gave me a boost and I became a real nerd then.

---

[5] *the German word "Sturm" means "storm"*

I finished the fourth grade with honours. It simply dawned on me, as they say. I decided to make something of myself. I was the poor son of a poor woman and always had the feeling that people looked down on me. And now I wanted to become someone who was respected..."

"To have power over others? At least that's how it was portrayed in the media at that time," I ask.

"What does power really mean? I just didn't want to stay 'down there'. As an unskilled worker who has to dance to somebody's tune. That's why I continued my education. Took courses. So that one day, I would belong to those who are asked for advice by others."

"How did it go from there?"

"I took care of everything myself after school. My mum wasn't doing so well economically at the time, and she was struggling after what she had experienced in her own life. Through the welfare service, I found a place in the Don Bosco[6] home in Linz. The director's surname was Teufel[7]. And that's just how he was like..." Josef F smiles ironically and goes on. "It was very strict there. We were young boys who liked to go to the cinema. But that was strictly forbidden! So, we secretly climbed out of the toilet window and ran to the cinema. It was only two hundred metres away from the home. There were four of us, me and three friends.

---

[6] *a home run by the Catholic Church*
[7] *the German word "Teufel" means "devil"*

Well, when we came back at about 10 p.m., we got caught. The director and his assistant stood in front of us and told us to pack up our things that same evening. The next morning after breakfast we had to move out.

That was a mess. There I stood, without an accommodation nor any money, because on top of that, I had been deprived of my apprenticeship allowance. I didn't dare go back to my mother. I hadn't seen her for three years and she wasn't doing well financially, either. I was really devastated at the time. I still tremble when I think about it. But again, I was lucky and got a chance. One of the friends who had been put on the street with me had an aunt at the magistrate's office who stood up for us. I found a new place to stay the same day, in an apprentice home in the Neue Heimat district of Linz. Then I really blossomed, also in sports. I was a well-trained lad and did a lot of sports, from handball to football to boxing. I played in midfield in football, as a striker, and I was good at shooting. I almost made it to the first league, but failed because of the medical examination. I was told I had 'too big a heart'! That surprised me, because I had never had any complaints, apart from the occasional stabbing chest pain." Josef F is so immersed in his past that he would have liked to go on talking for hours. But the officer behind the glass pane has just indicated to me friendly that the office hours are almost over. We have to call it a day. "I'll be back soon, anyway," I tell him encouragingly as we say goodbye.

Josef F:

Since it was summer, I also had to take care of our hotel in the Salzkammergut and the guests there. I organised excursions and hikes to show our beautiful country to our tourists and to entice them to come back. I also did not shy away from strenuous mountain tours. The most popular was hiking up the Schafberg, which demands a lot of fitness. A good part of our guests quit halfway up the mountain and stayed exhausted at the Eisenau hut. A small remnant bravely hiked on with me to the summit. The panoramic view from the hut landlord's terrace on top was magnificent, and a hearty snack was served as a reward. But the break was short-lived, we had to get back down to the valley quickly. There was a lot of activity in our inn in the evening, because our guests were very hungry and thirsty after the whole day of exertions. Sometimes I sat down with them and listened to their conversations. They were proud to have conquered their "weaker self" and would never forget this beautiful day in their lives. "I'll be back next year!" I heard more than once. Good!

***

The male guests mostly went fishing and came home late in the evening or at night. Their wives were bored, so I had to keep them entertained. I was happy to do it. I took them on excursions to Mondsee, Salzburg, St. Gilgen or Wolfgangsee, went shopping or visited a dance hall with them. They enjoyed it immensely, even though I was such a miserable dancer. You wouldn't think it possible how starved for affection and sex women can be when their husbands neglect them. Especially on vacation!

***

At the end of the season, I went home to return to my duties as a general agent. The market situation was excellent. Numerous customers had responded to my offers and were interested in the state-of-the-art, automatic production lines. Before they placed an order, they naturally expected a visit from me to discuss the details. This time, the tour would take me as far as Tyrol and Vorarlberg. That's where the financially potent customers were, but they did not spend their money lightly. The sales negotiations with them had always been lengthy, and this time, too, they would demand a lot of negotiating and persuasion skills from me. But I managed it! At the end of the business trip, I had three orders in my pocket, with a total order value of around 27 million shillings! That was a lot of money at the time. My persistence, constant market observation and, of course, my many years of professional experience had paid off.

Stein Prison, interrogation zone, in August 2022

"I get the impression that you are someone who always wants to have everything under control. Didn't that play a decisive role in your crimes?"

Josef F carefully folds the small note he almost always carries with him, only to spread it out again shortly afterwards and smooth it down with his fingers. He is usually never at a loss for an answer, has this question now unsettled him? After all, he knows that the psychiatric experts have attested that he has a pathological need for control, which is one of the severe personality disorders.

"You see where all this leads," he finally replies. "Think of values like family. It used to count as the nucleus of society. The parental home was the most important thing. Nowadays, everything is completely different. The state interferes everywhere. This leads to nothing good. I can see it here, where I am now: Many of those who end up in prison come from broken homes, grew up in shelters. These are breeding grounds for crime! The state can never replace the parental home. You can't imagine how often I see people here in prison who have gone off the rails because of severe upbringing deficiencies! They lose the bond with their family in prison for good and instead come into contact with crime and drugs! Those who are classified as 'mentally abnormal', like me, even get the 'measure'[8] on top of that and then stay in prison twice or three times as long! And once they stand in front of the prison gates after their release, they don't know where to go. They can't find work, because who would

---

[8] *a court-ordered placement in an institution for mentally abnormal lawbreakers*

hire a person with a criminal record? There is a lack of aftercare, the state does not have enough money for that. Failure is pre-programmed! It is a misery that is being hushed up. That really gets to me, because I see it here so often."

I believe his consternation. Driven by desire, longing for comfort and security, and pre-programmed failure are obviously prevailing issues in Josef F's life, which he also seems to reflect upon when observing his fellow inmates.

Josef F:

Inside, I understood the youth. I knew from myself how strong the urge for freedom and independence can be at this stage of life. The irrepressible need to get away from the monotony of everyday life. But I had kept myself in check, because I have always pursued a goal. I learned a profession and secured myself financially so that I wouldn't be taken advantage of by others later on. For others, however, the urge for freedom is like a scourge. They believe they have to fill their lives with adventure, pleasure and intoxication, which leads them straight into the abyss.

Stein Prison, interrogation zone, in August 2022

During my visits to the prison, we inevitably end up discussing all kinds of topics. For example, about my cat, which was ill at the time. I ask him if he has ever had any pets. Yes, when he was a child, a stray dog came to him. A black curly poodle. He liked him very much, because he protected him from his mother when she once again went after him. While he hid behind the pile of wood stacked in front of the fireplace, the dog had growled at his mother and chased her away. Unfortunately, a policeman had shown up one day and taken the dog away. He never found out what happened to him.

"I was sorry about the dog," he says with a sad expression. This episode from his life is an opportunity for me to ask him about his relationship with his mother.

Josef F:

"My mother raised me alone. She beat and kicked me until I lay on the floor bleeding. It made me feel so humiliated, so weak. (...) As a child, I always thought that I was unwanted (...) My mum was a maid, had to work a lot, I never got a kiss from her, and never a hug - although I tried so hard to make her treat me well. I was afraid of her, terribly afraid, of her unpredictability, of her beatings, of the kneeling on the edge of a piece of wood as punishment. And she was always calling me bad names, like Satan, criminal, a good-for-nothing. She forbade me to have friends..." These were the words used by the psychiatric expert Dr Adelheid Kastner in her expert report on the exploratory interview with Josef F.

***

Now, some fifteen years later, Josef F seems to have made peace with his mother. "She didn't have it easy. She had to work inhumanly hard. With the farmers, where she helped out with the sowing in spring and autumn, with the harvest. She had huge hands. I was afraid of them, because it really hurt when she beat me with them. I can still feel the pain today when I think about it…" But then he immediately defends her. "She was just alone and overwhelmed with me, because I was a very lively child. While she was away, she tied me to the table leg with a rope and left me alone. I tried to free myself. In the process, I pulled the heavy table over to the entrance, opened shutters of boxes and probably made a mess of things. She really didn't have it easy with me. But I'm sure she liked me in her heart. She just couldn't show it."

I can tell how much the topic moves him. "Tell me about your family. Where did your mother and father come from?" I ask him to distract him a little.

"I'll have to go back a bit to explain. I only know what I'm about to tell you from what my mother told me. My grandfather had an estate and a mill near Ardagger Abbey. He was very wealthy, but is said to have been brutal and hot-tempered. He was married, but his wife was unable to have children. So, he got the maids pregnant and had three children, a boy and two girls. One of them was my mother. My mum told me they all lived together on this big estate. Like an extended family. My grandfather's wife was said to be kind-hearted, unlike her husband. But he was rich. So rich that he was able to provide all his children with possessions. My mother inherited the house in Amstetten from him, where I later lived with my family as an adult. Back then, it was a large house with eight apartments. My mother then married a local transport entrepreneur. When there was still no offspring after two years, he filed for divorce, on the grounds that she was infertile. That must have offended my mum terribly. After the divorce, she wanted to find a new husband quickly and get pregnant at all costs. She was almost obsessed with having a child, so that she could get back at the transport entrepreneur! It happened with my father right away. She was already forty-two when I was born in 1935, her first and only child. Proof of her fertility!

The transport entrepreneur remained childless. He was the one who couldn't father children. That's what my mum told me again and again later."

"What was your relationship with your father like?" I ask further.

"You have to know, my father was a womaniser. He cheated on my mum all the time. She often complained to me that he had abandoned her. Especially during times when she was struggling financially. Much later in life, when I met my future wife, he tried to contact me again. Not directly, he probably didn't dare. But through my wife. 'A handsome guy, your father,' she said about him. Yes, he went down well with the women..."

"But as a father, he was more or less absent, I read," I enquire, and continue to ask. "What was his profession?"

"He was a train driver. And then, in the war, a fighter pilot. He was shot down and in 1945 taken as a prisoner by the

Russians. He came home after three years and demanded that my mother sign over half of the house to him. She strictly refused, saying 'That belongs to our boy!' Then he found someone else and moved out. It was very difficult for me not to have a father. As a child, I often longed for someone I could look up to and ask for advice."

"What did you live off?" I ask further.

"The house shed a little bit of money. During the war, there were two barracks in our area, where about five thousand soldiers were stationed. My mother gave them the opportunity to stay in her house with their wives..."

He grins. "There were already rumours that it was a house of pleasure. I still remember, I must have been three or four years old, when a soldier's girlfriend took me to her room. I was a snotty little boy and had no pants on, there was no money for that at the time. The woman lifted me up and said approvingly, 'This one will be a real man one day!' I was so ashamed and ran away. After the war, many refugees moved into the house. But the money wasn't enough, it was still paid in crowns back then, and the refugees didn't have anything anyway. So, my mother had to earn some extra money by helping out the farmers in the area. I was very much alone as a child. But I don't want to say anything bad about my mother. For example, she often spoiled me with pastries. Or got me books from the public library. I loved reading as a child. I liked Indian stories and adventure novels best, such as 'The Leatherstocking Tales'".

"I read that your mother was sent to the Mauthausen concentration camp when you were ten years old. Why?"

"Because she was against the Nazis. She got into it with a whole bunch of them, calling them 'Nazi scum'. That was all she had to say. They went berserk! They grabbed my mum, dragged her into an outhouse and tortured her terribly. One of them hit her so hard in the face that one of her eyes was crushed. I saw it hanging out, my God, I was so scared! I was there, but I couldn't do anything. She had surgery later on, but unfortunately the eye could no longer be saved. My mum was then deported to Mauthausen. When the Americans liberated the camp, she came back. But it was much worse with her then than before... Once, I got a very high fever. It was so sick that I almost died. Our neighbour came and pleaded with my mother to take me to the hospital as soon as possible... But I don't want to talk about all that today because I have long forgiven her. She didn't know any better, didn't know how to deal with me. She then withdrew from the public more and more, because she was embarrassed about the stitched-up eye. Maybe the rape was to blame, too."

"What rape?"

"Our house was in the Russian occupation zone. One evening, when she was on her way back from working at the farmers', a young Russian dragged her into his jeep and raped her. She managed to secretly take off his belt. His service number was written on the inside of the belt, so he could be traced later. He was then punitively transferred. I only found out about all this much later, from a neighbour. My mother didn't tell me about the rape, because she was ashamed. She started paying less and less attention to her appearance. In the end, she just walked around in torn clothes.

But she had once been a very beautiful woman, desired by many men. I had kept the countless love letters that her admirers had written to her. I hope my family didn't throw them away, it would be too bad. No, I really don't want to say anything bad about my mother. I have long since forgiven her for the beatings. She was all alone and had a very hard time. With me, too."

While his mother was in the concentration camp, ten-year-old Josef stayed with a foster family. As I researched later, he stole money for the train ride back to the bombed Amstetten to look for his mother. She had returned even more unpredictably after the liberation, beat her son and in the end no longer took any notice of him. As a child, he had once suffered from foreskin constriction and had not been able to urinate for days. It was only through the intervention of a neighbour that he was taken to a doctor[9].

A few weeks later, Josef F sends me the following letter describing his relationship with his mother:

"My mother's death did not come as a surprise to me, as she had long suffered from a mental illness and death was a release for her. Nevertheless, I suffered greatly from her loss. I realised that she meant more to me than what I had ever seen in her. She had simply been there for me when I needed her. Yet, she hardly ever received any thanks from me for her help. It was a quiet funeral with only a few mourners, as most of her acquaintances had already passed away or were unable to attend. It hurt me to see the lonely funeral procession behind her small coffin.

---

[9] *Source: Interview by Franziska Tschinderle with Dr Adelheid Kastner, published in "VICE" on 4 December 2014*

Afterwards, I went through a period of reflection in which I reviewed my memories of all the years with her. This period of reflection did me good.

It made my grief over my mother's death more bearable. However, there were still times when I felt the loneliness and abandonment particularly strongly. I then tried to suppress them, because I had no one to talk to about it. It took me a long time to really say goodbye to my mother. Even today, I think about her from time to time, and how she managed to keep us afloat with great hardship during the years of war turmoil. Although she always made it clear that I was an unwanted child, she loved me in her own way. She was very strict with me, and yet I had the feeling that she was well-disposed towards me. I hope she is doing better where she is now. She deserves it."

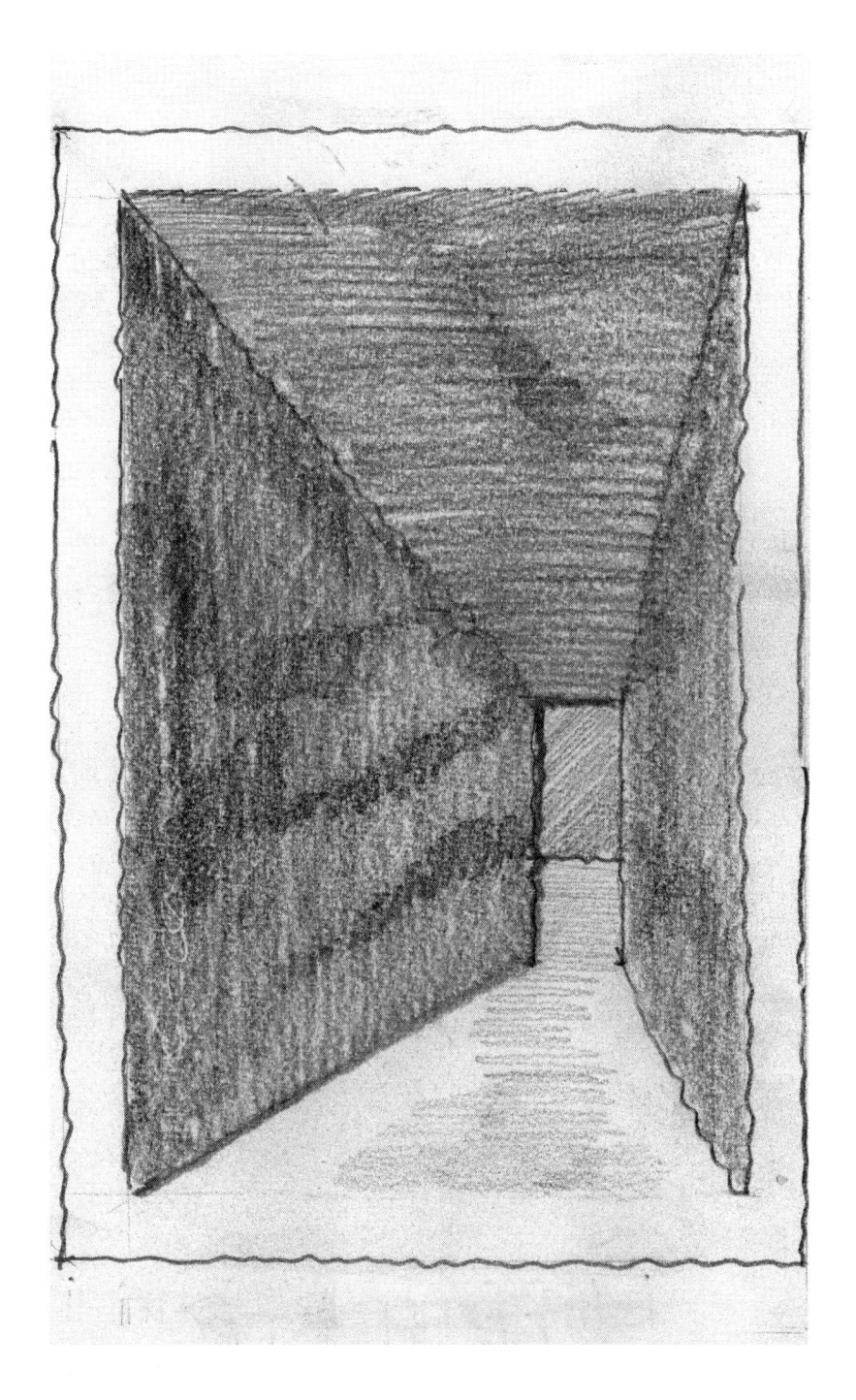

Josef F:

Winter came. I was alone at home and got up early that morning. The peace and quiet did me good, I felt free and could do whatever I wanted. I went up to the roof terrace. It was a bright day, the snow was glistening in the sun. I closed my eyes. Suddenly, I thought I heard children's laughter from a distance. I imagined a little girl frolicking in the snow. Her exuberant movements, shaking the snow out of her long blond hair. Suddenly, something grazed me hard on the upper arm and pulled me out of my daydream. It was a snowball. A child must have thrown it from the street onto the terrace.

I was full of anticipation for the evening ahead of me. The woman I would spend it with was attractive and craved tenderness. Especially now, when she had worries and was looking for comfort.

I met her many years ago at an event organised by a large construction company. A small mishap happened to me, spilling a glass of wine on her. She laughed and the conversation quickly got going. We soon realised that we were on the same page. Although she wasn't dressed in a pushy way at all and apparently wasn't looking for an affair, she turned me on. She kept a low profile, which spurred me on all the more to tell her about my varied life on the road. She was educated and spoke English and Italian fluently. As I later found out in our secret meetings, she was no longer desired by her husband. What a fool he was to neglect such an attractive, tempered woman!

***

We were lying in each other's arms in the hotel room. We had ordered two bottles of champagne and she was pouring out her heart to me. She had found out about her husband cheating on her again. I listened to her patiently. I knew she didn't love me, but as an understanding friend I was probably closer to her than anyone else. She appreciated my discretion and that I was good at listening and giving advice. It was already past midnight when she got up and ran a bath. I followed the temptation. We both lay naked in the water and let ourselves be carried away by the wild waves of passion. We spent the next day in splendid weather up on Linz's Pöstlingberg. As we parted, she hugged me tightly once more and showered me with wild kisses. "I'd like to go to Ghana with you," I spontaneously suggested. She reacted enthusiastically and did not even ask why I had chosen this particular country. She could not know that I had an ulterior motive: I wanted to meet my adult son, whom I had fathered twenty years ago during my professional stay there. What had become of him? His mother came from a wealthy family from the Ashanti tribe. A gifted painter, who could live well from her imaginative, colourful works. She had not needed to make financial demands on me and never did.

Stein Prison, interrogation zone, in August 2022

"When did you start wearing your moustache?"

"Oh, that was in Luxembourg. My job for the steel company had taken me there. There was a large construction site, for which I was technically responsible. I was twenty-four at the time, married and already father. I felt the responsibility that lay on me. The moustache made me seem more mature somehow. More serious. Perhaps that was the reason why I had grown it. We lived in a big bungalow that belonged to a wealthy family. And, guess what, the lady of the house fell in love with me! She was a very tempered and dashing woman. It was at a carnival ball. She pulled me to her without further ado and sat me on her lap. In front of her husband! Then, she invited me to her home alone and prepared an Austrian speciality just for me. Apricot and plum dumplings! They turned out very delicious. My mouth still waters now when I think of them. I have a sweet tooth, you know. They say the way to a man's heart is through his stomach. But it remained purely culinary, there was no sexual adventure. We had to pull ourselves together, because our spouses would certainly have found out about us... I think back with nostalgia to that great, lively woman. Perhaps she is stuck in my memory, because we left it just at that romantic flirt...".

Josef F:

It was a rainy Tuesday when we met at the Vienna-Schwechat Airport. My lover was exuberant with joy. Until the very end, she had doubts whether I was serious about inviting her on the trip. But I had kept my promise and booked a direct flight for both of us to Accra, the capital of Ghana. At home, I told the lie that I have to go to a faraway company for two weeks to assemble a complicated plant.

When we got off the plane after about seven hours, we were hit by hot and humid air. We called a taxi and went to the hotel to freshen up. In the hotel bar, I tried to reach my son's mother by phone. She was not available at the moment, so I left a message on the answering machine. She called me back late in the evening. I could tell from her voice that she was very happy about my arrival in her home country. She suggested that we go to her home town and check into a hotel there, and of course she would arrange a taxi for us. "We'd love to come," I declared with anticipation. Then I took my darling by the hand to go for a little evening stroll with her. To round up this beautiful day, we enjoyed a drink at the hotel bar. The following night was like a hurricane of passions. I had never thought it was possible for this woman to go to such lengths for me. Our carefree holiday mood, far away from professional and family obligations, probably had something to do with it.

The next morning, we were picked up by a chauffeur in an elegant Mercedes. The driver was on time and spoke German, which was very pleasant. Everything went very quickly, since we didn't have much luggage with us, because we wanted to buy clothes here. I knew that there were good and cheap tailors here who worked quickly.

Our journey took us along a bumpy country road, past roadside stands selling fruit and exotic dishes. When we arrived at the hotel after a three-hour drive, an excited crowd of people welcomed us. Although it had been more than twenty years, I recognised her immediately. Abena had put on just a little weight. I was the first to get out of the car and helped my darling out. The people were all speaking at once, and I couldn't understand anything in this babble of voices. Then Abena's resolute, distinctive voice rang out. She managed to silence the others immediately. She came over to me, embraced and kissed me passionately and exclaimed, "At last, I see you again! You haven't changed at all, maybe a little less hair. You look great!" I didn't have time to answer, because she was already hurrying into the hotel, where a long table with elaborate flower arrangements was set up for us. My darling and I were amazed at the splendour of this large room. No sooner had we taken our seats than the waitresses hurried over to take our orders. Abena sat next to me, and now I could finally ask her. "Where is my son? I don't see him anywhere..." She winked at me. "Edem is not fair-skinned like you, he is dark. But he is a handsome boy. And very hardworking and ambitious. He is about to finish his law degree and is already working for a lawyer. He sends his apologies, he still has an important meeting with a client. We can start with the food. I think he's also a little shy about seeing you, since he doesn't know you. He's dying for you to meet his girlfriend. I myself have long since embraced my future daughter-in-law in my heart. I'm sure you'll like her, too. She is studying medicine and wants to become a paediatrician." Then, Abena told me about her own life. She was still teaching at the university. My darling hardly got a word in, but she didn't mind. She enjoyed the beautiful ambience and the delicacies that were served to us.

Late in the evening, my son Edem finally arrived. I didn't recognise him, his mother had to introduce us. "Well, now you finally get to know each other in person. You do look a bit alike. The son is just taller than the father. That's good, so he can assert himself. Edem can be very dominant!" I could tell my son was uncomfortable with his mother praising him like that. I tried to ease his tension by asking him about his girlfriend. "She should come any time now. But you know how women are. When there is a special occasion, they need extra time," he replied, a little embarrassed. I chuckled and introduced him to my darling. He paid her a charming compliment. I could see that she liked him. In fact, my African son is an extremely attractive, tall young man with good charisma and a beautiful, free laugh. And by the way, he speaks excellent German.

His girlfriend arrived shortly before the big dinner. She was dressed in colourful traditional attire and was accompanied by two other young women, one prettier than the other. Her sisters, as I was told. She smiled gently at me while my son introduced her to me. Late in the evening, a big local band started playing. The people here had dancing skills in their blood and liked to party. My darling asked me to dance for the sake of politeness, even though she knew how much I loathed that. But African rhythms awaken emotional impulses and the urge to move in anyone who has even a little bit of temperament in their blood. Of course, I was not used to that and immediately started to *sweat. After only two dances, I had enough and went to the bar to order a refreshing drink. My lover continued to dance passionately. The hot music matched her temperament and I could tell from her flushed face how much she was enjoying herself here.*

While I was sitting at the bar, my son came up to me and took a seat next to me. He obviously wanted to talk to me, but it took a while to get the conversation going. After all, we didn't know each other. Gradually, I learned a few things about his life, which he could be proud of. In turn, I told him about my large family and showed him photos of his stepsiblings. Then his mother joined us. "But now it's my turn!" I couldn't refuse her and escorted her to the dance floor. The party lasted until the early morning hours.

Stein Prison, interrogation zone, in August 2022

"You were on the road a lot. On business trips, on holiday, even in faraway countries. Did you never think about your dark secret then?"

Josef F lowers his eyes as if my question had unsettled him. "When I was away, I pushed all my problems away. Including my secret. Everything was far, far away. I would have gone crazy otherwise! Only sometimes, when I was alone, I was haunted by dark thoughts. I immediately repressed them by distracting myself and thinking of something else…"

***

A sun-drenched street somewhere in the south. The sky above me is bright blue, the walls white-washed and lined with densely growing bougainvillea. Their intense scent mingles with the smell of the nearby sea. Suddenly, I feel a change. The brilliant colours fade, the flowers seem to wilt and emit a pale, musty smell. The ground beneath me begins to vibrate. I look down at my feet. They are standing on a manhole cover that is bulging upwards more and more. Startled, I jump to the side, and then I see them: black figures preparing to crawl out of the underground. At that very moment, I wake up.

The black figures symbolise the thoughts that Josef F entrusted to me. While he was on holiday in the sunshine of distant lands, he buried them deep in the bunker of his subconscious. But they kept occupying my mind, manifesting in bizarre dream sequences.

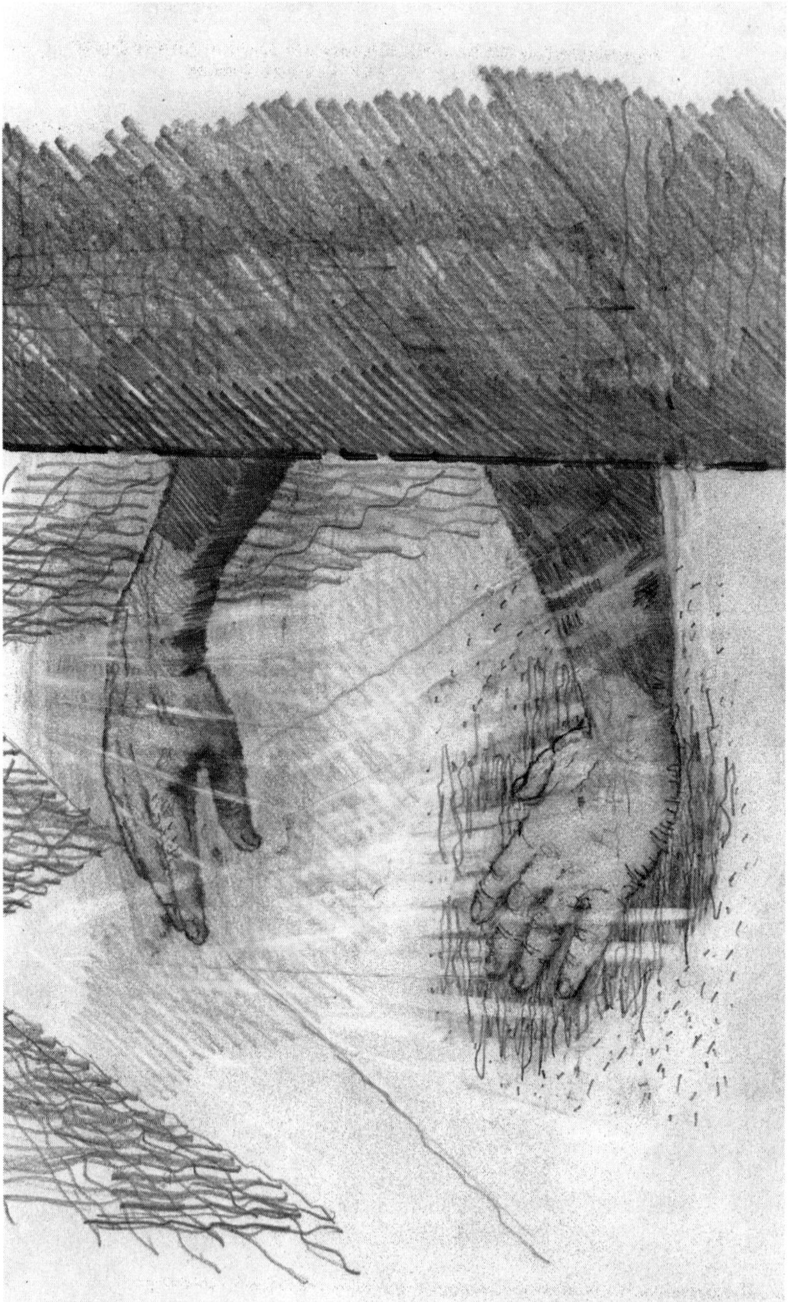

Josef F:

My two ladies spent the next day on a shopping spree in various exclusive shopping temples. I decided to keep to myself. After enjoying some excellent curry dishes in the city centre, I strolled back to the hotel for a nap. Beforehand, I had arranged with the reception to wake me up at 4 pm. I knew my lover's passion for shopping, she would certainly not be back before then.

I must have slept very deeply, because the maid had to really shake me awake. With a charming smile, of course, as exotic blossoms (sic!) are wont to do. As usual, she waited to see if I had any other needs, but this time I had two women with me. It was too risky for me to give in to my desire and leave traitorous traces. As soon as I was under the shower, the maid came back with a drink. She put it on the table and came into the bathroom. She asked me if she could help me, pointing to my back. I understood what she meant. She immediately set to work. Her gentle movements felt pleasant. If I had been here alone, I would have given in to my desire now. But I was there with my girlfriend and I had to renounce such tempting offers. I marvelled at myself that I could remain so steady. The maid smiled, although she was visibly disappointed. I gave her a generous tip though, and she left satisfied.

It was high time anyway, because after fifteen minutes my lover called me on the room phone: "Come to the bar, we're back!" When I saw the pile of shopping bags and boxes, I couldn't help myself saying, "You must have bought up half the town!" Both laughed, and Abena remarked, "Your girlfriend is so modest anyway. I would have bought a lot more. As a lonely woman, you have to comfort yourself with material things..." I protested. *"But you are an attractive woman. And, as I have noticed, very popular!"* Abena looked a little melancholic, as she opened up to me. *"I have met many interesting men in my life, but there was no one like you. But I have my son, whom I love very much. I have to tell you, he is like you. Stubborn, self-determined, freedom-loving."* I was so moved by her comment that I remained silent. And then, after a pause for thought, she added, *"And he is a seeker like you. This eternal search, this striving for a higher meaning will probably only be over when you have to say goodbye to life."* I will never forget those sentences. This woman, who had only accompanied me for a short part of my life, seemed to have penetrated into the deepest corners of my soul.

***

The next morning, my lover and I got up very early, because we had a long drive ahead of us. Our destination was an area several hundred kilometres away. I knew it because our company had set up a transmitting station there. There was a small lake in the immediate vicinity where crocodiles were cavorting. My lover couldn't miss that! Fortunately, Abena had left the chauffeur and car with us, because the roads were more than impassable and it could be very dangerous for a white person here. In case of an accident, there was a serious risk of becoming a victim to lynching.

We arrived in the early afternoon. The locals here had very different facial features from the Ashanti, and their skin colour was *jet black. But they were friendly and curious. While the chauffeur was getting food on my behalf for the crocodiles, we freshened up in the hotel room and changed to have lunch. On the hotel grounds, countless girls were loitering around to offer their sexual services. In a very natural, matter-of-fact way, which makes it a unique experience for a European. They prefer to stay overnight to enjoy the benefits of a shower, a bed and the cooling temperature of the hotel room.*

After a short nap, we set off in the Mercedes to the lake. Our driver had checked with the locals and knew a place where crocodiles could be encountered. When we arrived there, he pulled out the chicken. To my lover's horror, it was still alive. He waved it in circles and suddenly something moved on the shore. A crocodile hurriedly came ashore, climbed the steep bank and ran up the embankment. Immediately, the driver threw the chicken to the ground and took flight. For the crocodile had first snapped at him, the bigger prey! Fortunately, he was quick enough and the crocodile turned to the fluttering chicken, whose wings had been clipped. My lover covered her eyes, she could not watch. But I saw that she was observing the cruel spectacle between her fingers. The chicken was quickly eaten by the crocodile. Meanwhile, more crocodiles had reached the shore and were waiting for prey. The driver fetched two more fluttering chickens and threw them to the crocodiles. By now there were eight of them. A wild fight broke out between the crocodiles wanting the prey, and one of the chickens almost escaped. But the crocodiles were incredibly fast. We had more chickens to give, but spectators had gathered in the meantime who obviously did not agree with feeding the crocodiles. We preferred to quickly make our way home before there was any trouble.

The next day, we returned to the capital, where we spent a few more days on a beautiful beach lined with palm trees. The nights were uninhibited and wild. My lover kindled a fire in me that I would not have thought possible. She bit me during lovemaking, which spurred me on and degenerated a little into violence. That turned her on, encouraged her to even harder attacks, but due to my arousal I felt no pain. We fought together for the peak of arousal, racing towards an orgasm of superlatives. Later she told me that I had been the first and last man to awaken this deeply hidden, very special passion in her.

The holiday was gradually coming to an end. Abena asked me to have breakfast with her alone, which made me feel uncertain. What did she want to tell me? But she simply wanted an opportunity to finally spend some peaceful and quiet time with me. I found out that my return to Europe had saddened her back then and that she had wanted to hold me back. But in her culture, a man's decision was respected. In all those years, she was completely absorbed in her role as a mother. At the same time, she was also successful in her career, which is no contradiction in Africa. Children are part of life and are not excluded as they are in our society. But there was no room for another man in her life. Today I wonder, what would have happened if I had stayed in Africa back then?
A little later, Edem joined us. When he placed his order with the waiter, I gave him a sidelong glance. What a handsome, well-grown young man he had become. A son who has everything to make a father proud. Of course, I had to promise them both to accept the prompt invitation to his wedding.

The next morning, we went to the airport. The direct flight from Accra to Vienna-Schwechat was scheduled to depart at 10 a.m.

We had a small drink at the airport bar, but our flight was already called. The farewell was tearful. As we circled over the airport, I believed I recognised Abena and Edem as tiny dots on the observation deck. I was overcome by the oppressive feeling of leaving something that was actually much closer to me than what was waiting for me at home.

During the flight, I was seized by another anxious feeling. The last few weeks had been so colourful and full of events that I had hardly thought about my secret. Was everything still the way I had left it? Or had something terrible happened in the meantime? An accident? Had my secret been discovered? Was I even already on the alert for arrest in Austria?

After passing through the customs checkpoint at Vienna-Schwechat Airport, I breathed a sigh of relief. No one was looking for me. My lover and I were able to carry out our plan to spend another romantic love night in the airport hotel without any worries.

Stein Prison, interrogation zone, in September 2022

What do you appreciate in a woman?"

"I like it when she has temper. When she's approachable. I don't mean that in a sexual sense. I mean open-minded, in terms of her character."

"So, you like it when a woman takes initiative?"

He nods. "I was quite shy as a young person, you must know. It was at a dance..."

"Oh dear, nothing for you!" I remark with a wink, making him smile. "She was a blonde, delicate girl. She walked straight up to me and asked me to dance. Afterwards, she gave me a peck on the mouth. Well, that gave me a sting. I can still feel it today, my very first kiss...".

Josef F:

A lot of work had piled up at home. Fax orders, spare parts that had to be delivered quickly, customers who needed to be called back immediately. I never complained about the workload. I needed the tension and all the stress as a distraction from my real problems, which I had imposed on myself through my actions.

The next day, I set off at five in the morning towards Styria to meet an impatient customer. He had received a large order in the field of civil engineering that could not be handled with the machinery he had. He was overjoyed with my arrival and I was able to resolve all his concerns. He then invited me to lunch at a nearby inn. There, we also got to talk about personal matters. It was uncomfortable for me, but such things are part of deepening customer relations. He confided in me that his daughter had run away with a salesman a month ago, and since then he had not heard from her. His wife was under severe psychological strain as a result, was even thinking of suicide, refused any help and wouldn't let anyone come near her. I glanced furtively at the clock, time was pressing, but there was no end to his declaration of worries. I decided to take matters into my own hands by cheering him up. I ordered two more glasses of wine and then explained to him in a kind voice, "You know, you have to be patient with the youth. Your daughter is still very young. She will surely become sensible. Everything will be alright again!"

Relief spoke from his gaze as he said, "You are such a smart person. I thank you from the bottom of my heart for listening to me for so long!" If only he had known what a dark secret the person sitting opposite him held.
It became one of the biggest orders of my entire professional career.

Stein Prison, interrogation zone, in September 2022

I have been reading his manuscript for weeks now. Mostly in the evenings, after my appointments with clients. The parallel world that opens up before me generates quite contradictory emotions. It is difficult to escape them. This seemingly ordinary man unites so many contradictions in himself as hardly any other. He appears sympathetic, witty, obliging. And yet he has committed terrible crimes. He has taken the blame upon himself, but does not seem to be aware of the magnitude of its consequences. He writes of his longing for unique love, but describes countless fleeting affairs.

I decide to ask him about it. "Which woman would you say was actually the 'love of your life'? Was there one? Or someone you would call your soulmate?"

Josef F does not hesitate for long: "My wife. I always got along well with her. But we had very different spheres of life. I had my job, my travels, and of course my secret love affairs. I was always looking for adventure in some way. I guess I didn't appreciate her enough. Could you perhaps get in touch with her? I have so much to explain to her. They say that you should not only be at peace with yourself, but also with others before leaving this world…"

"Maybe later on, we'll have to think about that carefully. She might take it the wrong way, even feel pressured or threatened," I wave it off.

After a pause for reflection, he continues. "I have so much time to think here in prison. Now, through the conversations with you, things come flooding back. I would like to talk to my wife. I would like to know how she feels about me today. So much time has passed..." I look up from my notebook into a face that looks helpless and sad at the same time.

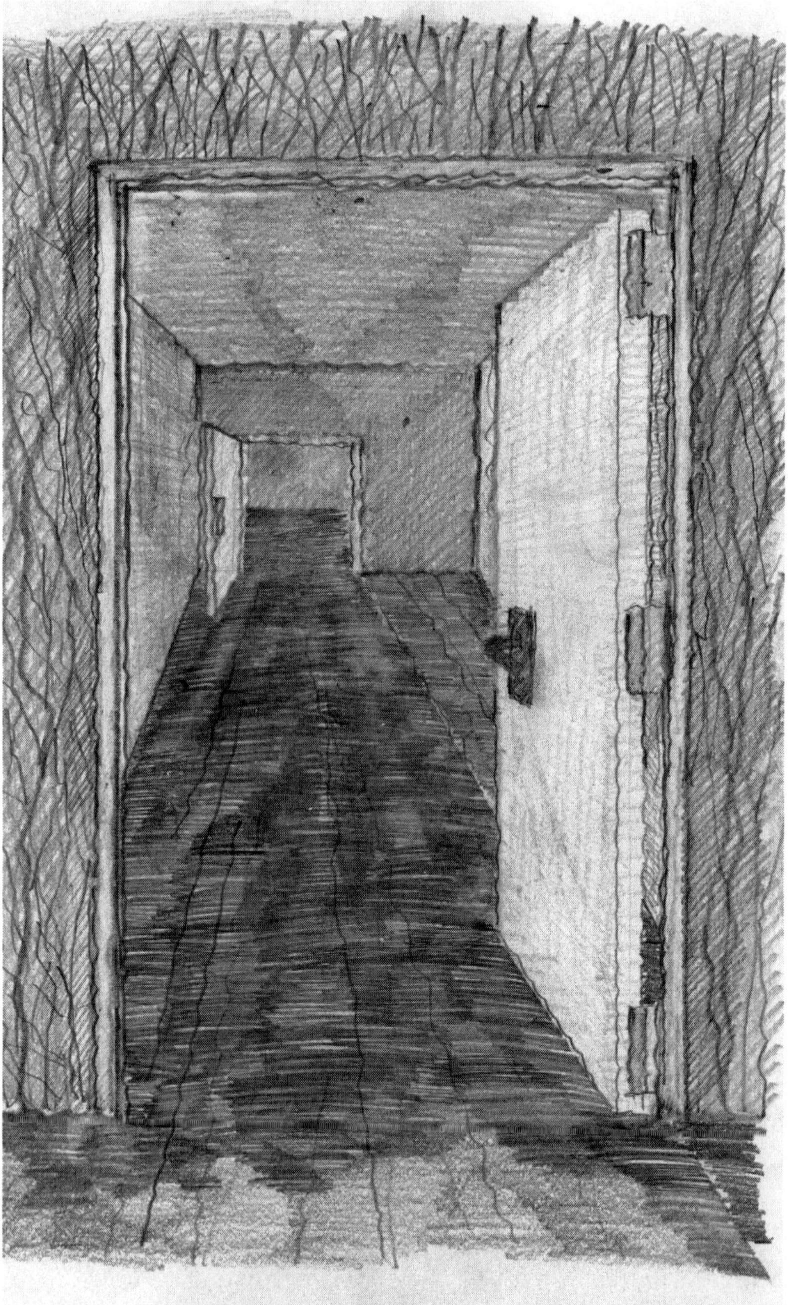

Josef F:

I went about my business as if in a trance. I was absent-minded and unfocused. Many thoughts were constantly circling inside me. What would happen to me? Should I blow the whistle? What would happen then? Prison, forced dispossession, financial ruin, disgrace! I began to think again about how I could best get out of the situation. But how could I? In sleepless nights, I imagined how the media would pounce on me. And unfortunately, not only on me, but on my whole family. Reporters would lie in wait for us, twist our words, write pages of reports about us. The fear that I would bring great shame on my family, that they would be defencelessly exposed to the media mob, it was almost unbearable.

My sadness could not be hidden from those around me. I was often asked about it and talked myself out of my professional worries. Far and wide, there was no one I could confide my fears and worries to. I felt infinitely lonely and lost. My job was the only lifeline to distract me. When a customer from Carinthia called me, because he urgently needed a spare part for an automatic control system, I immediately set off. The technical fault was fixed relatively quickly thanks to my expertise, but I still had to stay overnight. The trial run could only be started the next morning, because the required mixture of materials was not available immediately. The factory manager invited me to dinner, where we talked animatedly about technical innovations in production. It was getting very late and my eyes were already closing. Nevertheless, I was glad not to have thought about my worries for at least a few hours.

Stein Prison, interrogation zone, in September 2022

"Did you always want to have many children?"

"Well, I grew up as an only child, and suffered terribly from my loneliness. That's why I always wanted to have many children."

"And how do you see that now? If you went back to the beginning of your life, would you want to have a big family again?"

He shakes his head. "I would do everything very, very differently. But that kind of thinking is useless, because you are always wiser afterwards. Life teaches you many lessons. But by then it's usually too late to apply them."

Josef F:

In the late afternoon, I went out alone to our terrace. The pool was filled and the water was a brilliant blue. I took off my clothes and jumped in with a leap. The cool freshness made me forget everything around me for a brief moment. All the worries, problems and lies I had to keep telling my family.

Stein Prison, interrogation zone, in September 2022

In April 2009, the European Court of Human Rights (ECHR) upheld an appeal by the filmmaker Helmut F, who had been convicted of murder. The Court ruled that the overall exclusion of prisoners from the general right to vote, which was still in force at the time, violated the fundamental right to freedom of expression laid down in the European Convention on Human Rights (ECHR). As a result, Austria saw itself obliged to amend the law. Now, a person who has been sentenced to imprisonment no longer automatically loses his right to vote. Instead, according to the Austrian National Council Election Regulations, the court can revoke the right to vote in individual cases, in cases where a prison sentence of more than five years has been imposed. In practice, this hardly ever happens. However, the interest in participating in general elections in Austrian prisons is low. Partially also, but not only, due to the high proportion of foreigners who are not entitled to vote anyway.

The Federal President is newly elected in Austria in October this year.

"Did you vote?" I ask. Josef F nods. "Yes, of course I exercised my right to vote!"

"You don't have to tell me who you voted for, I was just curious whether-"

"The old man... I can't think of the name right now..."

"Van der Bellen?"

"Yes, I voted for him. I think he has proven himself. He should have done a bit more to curb corruption in politics. On the other hand, what can he do in his position? I voted for him because I don't think he did anything wrong."

Josef F gives me the impression that he is no longer interested in everyday politics. People like him usually choose the tried and tested and shy away from change. In addition, there is no access to the internet and its wealth of information in Austrian prisons, at least not officially. Incidentally, this is accompanied by very practical problems: orders for clothing, electrical appliances or other commodities that are not available in the prison itself, can only be ordered via catalogues. Most companies, however, stopped sending out such catalogues a long time ago.

Josef F:

The Christmas holidays were approaching relentlessly. I loved decorating the huge Christmas tree in our living room. It had to be really cheesy, with colourful Christmas balls, tinsel and, of course, star sprinkles to make the children's eyes light up on Christmas Eve. The scent of gingerbread, cinnamon and oranges was so promising in the house. Back then, it still snowed frequently in winter, and the snow-covered landscape was inviting for walks in the cold, fresh air. On the way, you would encounter horse-drawn sleighs, accompanied by the delicate sound of bells, muffled by the thick blanket of snow. That was the magic of the Christmas season, as I had loved it. But over the years, this magic gradually disappeared. The hectic pace and shopping stress in overcrowded shops shaped everyday life. Values like family, peace and contemplation lost their meaning. I longed for a place where I could escape from all that. A place where I could be myself again. A place of absolute peace.

Stein Prison, interrogation zone, in September 2022

"I noticed in your manuscript that you keep writing about Christmas and birthday celebrations with your family. What was that like in your childhood?"

Josef F shakes his head. "There was no Christmas for me. No Christmas tree, and certainly no presents. We had no money for such things. And birthdays? No, we never celebrated them. My mother had to make sure we had enough to eat."

"Did that make you sad?"

"Certainly. But there were people who helped us. Like my friend Karli and his parents. They were quite wealthy, they owned a clothing shop in Amstetten. They once bought me a cake for my birthday. Or gave me clothes as a gift. I even got shoes once. I still remember walking barefoot in April. My shoes were so worn out that you could see my bare toes. The ground was so cold that it really hurt! And then a dog of a handicapped man bit me in the butt... No, it was not a nice childhood." These are certainly painful childhood memories that Josef F speaks of, and yet it seems to do him good to talk about them.

"It was simply the post-war period," he continues. "Our town was occupied by the Russians. There were many rapes, also in our house. I can still see what it looked like back then, the bullet holes from the machine guns. But the Russian soldiers were nice to us children, they spoiled us with money and sweets. I also learned a bit of Russian, especially how to swear."

"What did your mother call you when you were a child?"

"She called me Pepperl. Or Rotzpipp'n[10] when I had done something wrong again..." Suddenly Josef F starts to cry, but quickly pulls himself together and continues. "My mother certainly didn't have it easy with me. At the age of ten or twelve I had become a real rascal. I was in a gang that fought against other gangs with wooden swords. I was a strong boy and felt like a real robber chief. We ran around in the woods and caught fish from the Ybbs river with our bare hands. My mum then fried them.

The police visited her not only once because of my pranks and truancy. I was simply missing a father. I mean a role model I could look up to. But then the teacher Sturm came. I will never forget that name. He believed in me and didn't give up. That's how he succeeded in awakening my ambition. I firmly resolved to acquire knowledge and make something of myself."

---

[10] *Austrian variation for "Rotzbub" [snotty boy]*

At a regional court in Lower Austria in October 2022

His name was Liam. The owner had been looking for the pretty, black and white spotted border collie for days, posting appeals on social media. Then they found him: dead in a well shaft. The perpetrator had inflicted unimaginable suffering on the animal. Liam's legs had been tied, his muzzle had been taped shut with parcel tape, and then thrown into the well, where he suffocated in agony. The owner arranged for an autopsy and did everything in his power to find the culprit. In the end, his own partner was charged.

I had always sworn to myself: "I will never defend an animal abuser in court!" The moral outrage of animal rights activists at my decision to do so is great. But my client swears her innocence.

The main hearing is at a regional court in Lower Austria today. Due to its unusual cruelty, the case is particularly close to my heart. But as always, I fight professionally and with the greatest possible commitment for my client. She seems highly nervous; her hands clenching a paper tissue. The black and white pictures of the helplessly bound animal and the gloomy shaft lie on the judge's table. It quickly becomes clear that the judge does not want to believe the defendant. He sentences her to a conditional prison term of a few months. A much higher sentence is not possible anyway, as the penalties for animal torture are still comparatively moderate. "The evidence speaks against you!" he justifies his verdict. As I leave the courthouse, the tension falls away and only then I realise the parallelism: this was also the court where Josef F was sentenced to life imprisonment for his heinous crimes.

Josef F:

In the meantime, the market was saturated with production equipment for the concrete industry, so I had to look for new products to offer. I decided to visit the big trade fair for building construction and civil engineering in Hanover. I had established an excellent reputation in the industry. My main focus was on automatically controlled bucket conveyors for feeding production machines and complete mixing plants. My company had its own exhibition stand in Hanover, with a demonstration model for customers.

The business trip was very demanding, as I had to look after customers all over Austria. There wasn't much time for evening celebrations, as I had to be at the stand at eight o'clock the next day to prepare everything for the rush of customers. After a week, I was able to sum it up: I had landed many orders, my persistent efforts had paid off. I was in high spirits.

Stein Prison, interrogation zone, in October 2022

"All sorts of things have been written about you. It said somewhere that you went to prostitutes, or have been in swingers' clubs?"

Josef F shakes his head vehemently. "What nonsense! Never in my life did I go to a prostitute, and never to swingers' clubs. That doesn't suit me at all. I've always been a late bloomer in love. It takes me some time to warm up to a woman. I need my start-up time before having sex..."

Josef F:

I don't hide the fact that I also used my various trips to cultivate female acquaintances. They were almost always married or in relationships, often with jealous men. One of the ladies was just at the dangerous age of 36, her husband nineteen years older and away on an installation job. I had known her for many years and casually called her up. "I happen to be in your neighbourhood soon, we could meet up briefly..." We arranged to meet at an inn at Lake Mattsee. She came in a fancy red Mercedes convertible. Of course, she longed for more. I had taken the precaution of booking a room. After she had put down the luggage, she immediately started undressing. She still had her dream figure. Then she went to take a shower, and I wanted to follow her. But I didn't want to rush things. I knew she liked to take the lead and could be passion personified, leaving treacherous marks on your body...

She swept me away into a swirl of passions. She was an athletic, well-trained woman and as agile as a snake. It wasn't easy to fend off her almost aggressive outbursts. She was the one who determined the rules of the love game. Later we strolled along the lake. I took in the wonderful scenery of the landscape and the people enjoying themselves on the beach while she told me about her life. It wasn't all good things. Her husband had caught her in adultery and beaten her black and blue. Now they lived separately and got along better. They had agreed that they would each do for themselves. But she knew that he still controlled her despite this agreement. In the evening, we went to a dance at the inn where we were staying. Since, as is known, I was not much into dancing, we retired to the room after midnight with a bottle of champagne.

The next morning, I was incredibly exhausted. And yet more relaxed than I had been in a long time, because the sexual excursion had done me good.

Stein Prison, interrogation zone, in October 2022

"Would it be possible to keep a hamster here in prison?"

"Never! Locking up someone innocent, that's out of the question!" is the prompt reply. Is that sarcasm now? I have long been aware of Josef F's tendency towards cryptic humour. "But just imagine, once I actually had a bat in my cell. I don't know where it came from. The officer discovered it on the wall. 'What have we got here, that's not allowed!' he exclaimed."

"What did you do with the bat?"

"I took it off the wall and put it into a shaft leading outside. It was still quite small, probably a young one."

In the past, it was not uncommon for prisoners to keep animals. Mice, hamsters, even cats. Today, inmates at Stein Prison are allowed to have an aquarium, at most. Nevertheless, animals find their way into the old walls again and again[11]. Pigeons, for example, fly through the cell windows, because there are inmates who feed them. As a result, they lose their natural shyness towards people and sometimes get into cells, where they are less welcome.

---

[11] *In the historical part of Stein Prison, there was a convent of a strict women's order, the Redemptorist Sisters, until 1848*

Josef F:

In January, my company sent me to a two-week sales conference in Copenhagen, where new production equipment was presented. I also had to give a presentation there, which I had prepared well based on market analyses and plans.

I drove to the airport at dawn and parked my car in the parking garage. Since I was too early, I strolled around, got some alcoholic beverages and tobacco products for my Danish colleagues, and read through my presentation. Before I went to the gate, I skimmed a few newspapers. So many criminal cases, accidents, human tragedies. I felt a twinge when suddenly two policemen appeared. Were they patrolling because of me? I tried to reassure myself. Before I left, I had as always meticulously checked several times that everything was perfectly secured. No one would be able to discover my secret during my absence.

It was a quiet flight in beautiful weather. The export manager was waiting for me at the exit in Copenhagen and greeted me warmly. We waited for the arrival of a colleague from Finland and drove to the hotel. There was a lot of fish and alcohol for dinner, and so the very first evening ended in a drinking binge. The Danes proved to be extremely hard-drinking companions I made sure I could slip away to my room as inconspicuously as possible, for tomorrow would be a hard day and I was one of the first to have to give a presentation.

The next day, a typical Danish buffet full of delicacies awaited me in the hotel's breakfast room; flour dishes, countless types of cheese and sausage, eggs and so on. I was glad that I had left on time the evening before so I could fully enjoy this! The other representatives gradually came with tired expressions on their faces and only drank coffee or tea. The bus arrived on time at 9 and took us to the main plant in Ringstedt where the convention took place.

Even before the official part began, the company owner expressed his gratitude for the successful efforts in the individual countries. There had been record sales last year, and he specifically highlighted the extremely respectable performance of little Austria. Of course, this would be rewarded in the form of a premium increase. For next year, a 14-day trip to Brazil for Carnival, including a stay in a five-star hotel, was promised to the best salesman.

The presentations, conferences and demonstrations lasted a week. I was happy when the first clients arrived on Saturday. A total of eighty customers from numerous countries were expected to attend. They were interested in the new technological developments on the market. They were guided through the factory halls, where they also learned a lot about the origins and the company's goals. The highlight was the demonstration of the state-of-the-art bucket conveyor. The construction manager ceremoniously pressed the start button, and the automatic process began to run according to programme, emptying the concrete mixture into the plant containers. It didn't work right the first time, which made the company management a little nervous. However, the second test run succeeded impressively and everyone applauded. Of course, we also took an extensive excursion into the exciting Copenhagen nightlife in the evening.

After two weeks, the bus took us back to the airport. Back in Austria, I rushed through the Friday traffic as fast as I could.

Somehow, a strange restlessness had taken hold of me, almost like a premonition.

Stein Prison, interrogation zone, in October 2022

By now, I am deeply immersed in the manuscript. I find myself in the midst of Josef F's strange worlds. The one on the surface seemed bright and cheerful, he played the role of the decent family father perfectly. Underneath, however, lay his other, secret world: dark, unfathomable, shady, almost unreal. This world, hidden deep inside him, was probably the one that corresponded to his true nature.

I have long suspected that the key to Josef F's committed acts lies in his early childhood. "I was impressed the other day when you told me about your childhood and youth. How precise your memories still are. That you still remember all the names…" I know from my grandmother that, in old age, events and abilities from long ago seem to become reawakened. She came from the Burgenland wine town Gols, which had belonged to Hungary in her childhood. When she was approaching one hundred, she preferred to speak to her Hungarian nurse in the nurse's mother tongue.

Josef F often talks about his mother, again now, and always emphasises, "I liked her very much". Even though she often treated him brutally. "When she hit me, I immediately fell to the floor. In the end she looked really "schiach" [12], with her

---

[12] *a colloquial Viennese expression for something very ugly or hideous*

eye knocked out. She was also missing two fingers." When I ask, I find out that she got her hand caught in a chopper when she was a child. Josef F goes on to talk about fond childhood memories. "My mum spoiled me with lots of sweets. It was nice when we went to the farmers together, to fence..." When he sees my perplexed face, he enlightens me. "Yes, fencing. That's what we called it when we knocked on the farmers' doors and begged for a piece of bread, bacon, or an egg." I had never heard that expression before. "But she wasn't happy at all when I joined the Red Hawks. The 'red brood', they are all good-for-nothings, she scolded them."

"How did you come to join the Red Hawks," I ask.

"I was looking for connections with people my own age. I also liked the uniforms. The beautiful blue shirt, the red neckerchief, that was very dashing. And, of course, the sport! I learned handball there. I have always been very sporty. Later I joined the ATUS, the Workers' Gymnastics and Sports Club. I met my first love at the 'Red Falcons'."

"You must tell me more about that," I enquire.

"Her name was Luzi. She was dark-haired, a completely different type than my later wife, who is blond. And very funny and spirited. She always wanted to give me kisses, but I was too cowardly. I was just so shy back then. I didn't know about tenderness and all that. My mother never caressed or kissed me. And then someone else came along and gave Luzi a kiss! And that was it for my first love, I was very disappointed. Later I lost track of her, because I went to Linz for the apprenticeship."

"And how were you actually enlightened?"

"Not at all. That's just how it was back then, there were no sex education classes or anything like that. But when I was eight years old, I was already curiously looking at girls and 'playing' with the girls from the neighbourhood..."
"You mean what they call 'doctor games'?"

He laughs. "Exactly. We just showed each other what we had down there... But I always shied away from a kiss. Because I never got one as a child."

Josef F:

That night, I had a beautiful dream. I was with a woman on our roof terrace. She only had a bathrobe of flowing white silk on. Light-footed, she walked to the edge of the pool, dropped her only piece of clothing, and slipped into the water. Her slender body moved in it as gracefully as a mermaid. Her blond, loose hair contrasted beautifully with the azure water.

In my law office in October 2022

A number with a Graz area code appears on the display of my mobile phone. I immediately assume it is a prison inmate. Calls from prisons are centrally coordinated by a telephone company in Graz. In order to be able to make calls, the inmates have to get prepaid cards charged. The calls are made via landline phones that are mounted on the walls in the individual units. I don't recognise his voice at all, it sounds completely different on the phone. Younger, brighter. When I tell him this, he remarks mischievously, "Good to know, I can play pretend sometimes." Then he asks me not to come on Wednesday, because he has a therapy session. We reschedule the appointment.

In the meantime, I have reached those parts of his manuscript where perversion and criminal sophistication blended into crimes of unimagined dimensions.

Josef F:

I had played the role of the surprised family father who took responsibility perfectly well. The next morning, I got up at five o'clock. There were all kinds of things to do. I went to the gendarmerie, where a protocol was typed up. I signed it and that was that. No questions, no enquiries, and certainly no involvement of the public prosecutor's office. I had not imagined it would be so easy. In fact, I had already imagined how a police squad would storm our house, question the tenants and at last unravel my secret...

**

I had neglected my job somewhat because of the stirring recent events. The next morning, when I wanted to go to the flat quickly after breakfast, I heard my secretary rushing up the stairs with clattering steps. She always wore elegant high heels, even at work. I liked that and would have liked to get closer to her, but I knew she was firmly taken. She was so out of breath that I would have loved to take her in my arms and calm her down. But it was about an important business matter. A customer had complained that his system had not been working for a week and I had to go there as soon as possible. I called right away and got an unparalleled telling off. The angry customer shouted so loudly that I had to hold the receiver half a metre away from my ear, otherwise my eardrum might have burst! When he had calmed down to some extent, I had the problem explained to me. I knew my equipment by heart and therefore found the fault immediately. Quickly, I packed the necessary parts, got into my car and drove towards Salzburg to the customer.

When I arrived, I had the machine operator describe the fault to me again in the presence of the production manager. I had brought the right parts with me and after a few manual operations, the system was working perfectly again. The customer was highly satisfied and apologised for his inappropriate behaviour on the phone. On the way back, I did my planned bulk shopping. It was almost midnight when I finally arrived home. In the garage, I set about loading and putting away a full seven wheelbarrows full of goods. Then I fell into bed, dead tired.

Stein Prison, interrogation zone, in October 2022

"That shirt looks good on you!" I mean it. The gold-brown-black striped shirt forms an elegant contrast to his white hair and pale, finely wrinkled skin. "Oh, I've had that for a long time," he answers casually, but I can tell he is pleased with my compliment. I have managed to read up on all his women's stories and can well imagine what made him so successful with the opposite sex; Josef F is someone you like to talk to. He is witty and talkative, but then also stops himself. "I'm not keeping you, am I, doctor?"

I ask him if there are any childhood photos of him. Unfortunately not, he left everything behind. The house was auctioned off, the family scattered to the four winds.

Later, on the way home to Vienna, I choose one of my favourite songs from Spotify, "Dust in the wind…". The song was first published in 1977 by the US-American rock band "Kansas". I was fourteen at the time and, due to the dramatic events around the "German Autumn", I was "politically awakened", so to speak. In my naive longing to break out of my bourgeois world, I distanced myself from the "disco" wave, perceived as "shallow". Instead, I sympathised with the criminal gang of the "Red Army Faction"[13]. Fortunately, this youthful aberration had no consequences.

---

[13] *The Red Army Faction (RAF; German: "Rote Armee Fraktion"), in its early stages commonly known as Baader-Meinhof Group (or Baader-Meinhof Gang), was a West German far-left militant group*

But that is also a reason why I do not presume to make any rash judgements about others and their actions. Incidentally, Winston Churchill once said: "He who is not a communist in youth, has no heart." As the late summer landscape of the Wachau passes me by, I indulge in a strangely melancholic mood.

In one of the law firms in which I once did my training, there were many files of persons who were under "guardianship", as it was called at that time. These were people who were mentally incapable or no longer capable of looking after their own affairs. When they died, I not only took care of the legal matters, but also organised the clearing of their flats. Among all the belongings, there were always lovingly compiled photo albums and folders with letters. It was my job to hand everything over to the clearance service. "All we are is dust in the wind..."

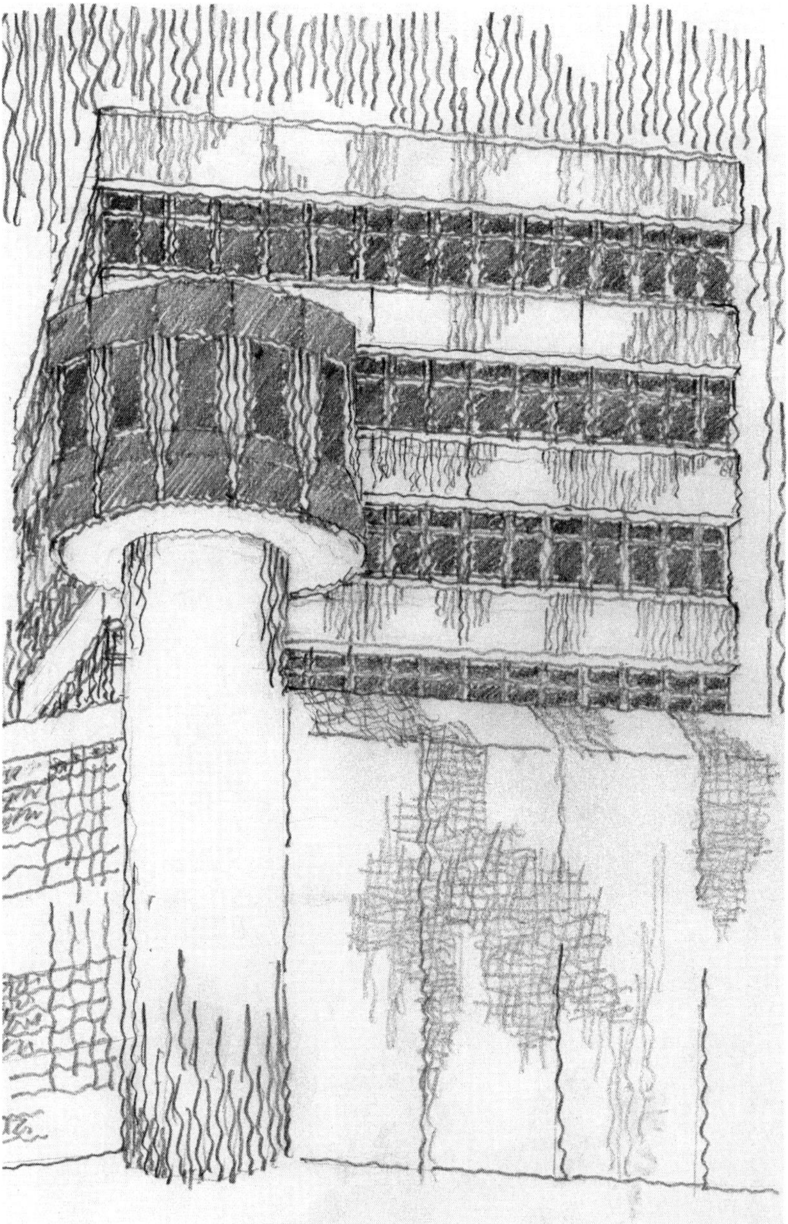

Josef F:

Her identity is not relevant, so I won't reveal where she came from and how she came into my life. In any case, she came just in time, when things were very challenging for me both privately and professionally, and she caught me up. She was attractive, open-minded, intelligent and decades younger than me. It had started with a few fleeting encounters. She was responsible for complaints in a company, and she settled everything to my complete satisfaction. This time, too. Her charming smile made me forget my worries for a moment. When I thanked her, she looked at me for a moment too long. She wrapped up her invitation to dinner in a clever remark. "A little variety is always good. Not just with food..." I couldn't resist her charm and agreed. It was touching how she had made an effort; elegant glasses, rose petals scattered over the tablecloth, flickering candlelight. She couldn't know that I didn't like semi-darkness while eating. I like to see what's being served on my plate. It turned out to be a feast for the senses, because she had conjured up one of my favourite dishes, pork chops with fried egg and pineapple. We drank excellent red wine with it. The alcohol loosened my tongue and she found out a lot about me and my life.

Dessert followed, the sight alone was a treat: ice cream pancakes with whipped cream, sprinkled with chocolate icing. Then she got up to get the champagne. Suddenly, I felt hot. She snuggled up to me like a cat and breathed into my ear, "It can get late tonight, because I'm off work tomorrow... I'm going to take a shower." With that, she had me, the older, experienced man, hunted down like a prey.

She got out of the shower and simply took my breath away. She had a seductive figure and knew how to show it off. She wore nothing but a see-through baby-doll dress with a neckline that reached down to her navel. When she bent over, her breasts popped out and pressed against my face. I felt a throbbing heat, my pulse was racing, I was done for. But she went on mercilessly, bent lower and gave me a long French kiss. "Now you can take a shower, too. Hurry up, I've already prepared everything," she whispered. Out of the corner of my eye I saw that she had a bath towel with her, which she threw on the corner bench. Sleep was out of the question that night. The next morning, I saw that the bath towel had bloody stains. She then revealed to me that she had still been a virgin. "I kept it from you so as not to frighten you!" I felt honoured to have been chosen by this young, beautiful and passionate woman to spend her first night of love with. "I knew you weren't as cold as you pretend to be! It was wonderful with you. It's a pity you're married," she then said. We agreed that our affair would remain a secret. "This is between the two of us and no one else's business. It will remain our secret," she affirmed.

***

The following evening, I was late because of a business appointment, so she had to warm up the food. Nevertheless, it tasted delicious. She had already changed and was wearing a gauzy minidress. The discreet neckline gave a pleasant insight into the sweet fruits in the basket. Considering that she had been a virgin only a few hours ago, she knew perfectly well about how to turn men on. *After finishing our diner, we went to the bathroom without a word, where she ran a bath. She bent over the edge of the bathtub provocatively, my gaze caught her charms, my passion skyrocketed. She was quickly undressed and I followed her into the water. Immediately, she began playing her games, a real talent. She had many tricks up her sleeve on how to ignite my passion and stamina in lovemaking… I spent the whole night with her.*

Stein Prison, interrogation zone, in October 2022

"You have been 'retired' here at Stein Prison for a year now. What kind of work did you do in prison before that?"

"I've been a houseworker for fourteen years." A houseworker is responsible for everyday tasks such as distributing food, mail, and cleaning. Accordingly, you get around a lot in prison.

"So, you often had contact with other inmates?"

"Yes, and I got along very well with all of them. That is still the case. I get on well with both the officers, with a few exceptions, and my fellow inmates. I am popular. That is also noted in my file. The older I get, the more I get served here. I actually don't like that at all. I've always been one to do things myself."

"You get served here? Do you mean by the inmates or the officials?"

Josef F laughs uproariously. "Of course from the other inmates, not from the officers! There's nothing like that here, that would be something!" Now I also have to chuckle about my naive question. Even people who, like me, have been confronted with the world of prison from the outside for decades, cannot really put themselves in the shoes of prisoners. To understand what it really means to have lost values like freedom, self-determination and probably also a piece of human dignity.

"Are there inmates with whom you are close?"

"I get along quite well with Alfred U. Just recently, there was a TV programme about his case. Journalists are so hungry for sensationalism; they just can't get enough. Ugh!"

Alfred U, who is now 68 years old, is a former client of mine. He has gone down in criminal history as the so-called "sea killer". After being imprisoned for more than thirty years for violent and sexual offences, he was released on parole. After only two years, he relapsed. He strangled a prostitute, dismembered her body and sunk parts of it in Lake Neusiedl. Other body parts were found in his freezer, where he had frozen them minced with beef in order to "taste them", as he put it. In 2019, he was sentenced to life imprisonment and sent to an institution for mentally abnormal offenders. He is serving his sentence in Stein Prison, where he works as a skilled printer in the prison print shop. He is also an enthusiastic cook and has already given me two self-written cookbooks as a gift, printed in Stein Prison.

"Alfred U is always hanging around in our kitchen, preparing huge quantities of schnitzels and pastries, it's crazy. He often asks me to help him. But I don't like that at all. I don't want to get fat. I've always watched my figure!"

As part of the so-called residential sub-unit, the inmates have their own kitchen rooms where they can prepare meals for themselves or other inmates from the ingredients they have bought.

"Do you miss being a houseworker, because you get around less now?"

"Yes, on the one hand I miss the work. But on the other hand, I'm also happy because I can look after myself more now. In order to stay fit and slim, I do gymnastics three times a day, especially for my legs."

"What does your daily routine look like?"

"I get up at 5 a.m. every day. The first thing on the agenda is personal hygiene. Then I start preparing a hearty breakfast. Coffee, ham, eggs, butter, buttermilk or curd cheese. Protein is important at my age. Honey or jam to go with it. At the moment, I'm enjoying an excellent orange marmalade. I spend quite some time eating breakfast, up to two hours. It's a real ceremony. I also read the magazines I have ordered and cut out what interests me. I want to stay informed. I'm going to need some things when I get out of prison. It's good if I'm prepared and have everything together. Afterwards, I do some physical training, gymnastic exercises. I exercise a lot more now than I used to when I was a houseworker."

"And what else do you do during the day?"

"Writing, mostly. It's going a bit slower at the moment, but I got another eight pages done. It's interesting how memories of long-ago events come back. For example, I've just become aware of how often I've been involved in serious, often fatal accidents at work. And how lucky I was that nothing happened to me! I still remember how a worker was crushed by a crane right before my eyes. It was in Schwechat, we were putting up a tanker for forty million litres of oil. The worker forgot to tighten the clamps on the crane, causing the cable to slip and the crane to swing to the right. I got away just in time, but the poor guy was hit by the crane. Another time, there were two fatalities at once. It was at a tank farm in Lobau. One of the workers who had been happily cycling to work that morning, was literally decapitated by a torn-off metal cover. Things can happen so quickly..."

"And now you lead such a quiet life," I remark, to keep the conversation flowing.

"Yes, it's basically the same thing every day. Except for Wednesday, I have my psychotherapy on Wednesday. I've also become a bit of a gardener, it's very calming. Someone has given me a beautiful Christmas star, I hope it doesn't die on me. Like the lemon tree did back then. My cell is quite sunny, though."

"And what about going out in the courtyard, you need to get some fresh air, don't you?"

"No, I don't go out. It's too dangerous for me. Who knows who I might meet there. Besides, I have a big window, it's open day and night. I go to the window and take deep breaths. I do real breathing exercises. Unfortunately, for some time now they have been putting the rubbish bins right under my window. In the summer, an unbearable stench develops, then I unfortunately have to close the window."

"And what about the commissary?"

Once a week, the inmates have the opportunity to spend the money they earn on everyday goods at the "commissary". This is a kind of shopping centre in prison. It is located in a larger hall in Stein Prison. However, the goods cannot be taken out freely; they have to be ordered from the staff.

"I haven't been going there for six months. It has become too tedious for me to go there. Another inmate has been doing that for me. I write down anything I want from there for him." Then he adds mischievously, "The ladies from the sales staff downstairs are a bit disappointed anyway, they've already asked for me a few times: 'But where is Mr F?'"

The time has passed far too quickly during our conversation, I have to call it a day. "Please give my regards to Mr U, I would like to thank him very much for the second cookbook," I ask him as a farewell favour. He promises me to do so and wishes me a safe journey home.

Josef F:

In autumn, I went on an extended business trip to visit my clients. A secret no one was allowed to know: My young lover accompanied me. Some customers thought she was my secretary and were very fond of her. One of them even said that he would order from me more often now just to hear her beautiful voice on the phone. We also went on short hikes in wildlife parks and attended dance events together, at which, as usual, I didn't cut a particularly good figure. But young and carefree as she was, she laughed boisterously at my helpless attempts. And yet, the affair was gradually becoming tiresome for me. I knew we had no future due to the big age gap. I wished that she would soon find a suitable partner. Young, pretty and spirited as she was, that should not be a problem for her. At the end of our journey, I took her home and we agreed not to see each other for the next few days. I also wanted to see for myself whether I could manage without her. And that's how this short-term affair ended before it had even really begun.

Stein Prison, interrogation zone, in October 2022

"When you think of your former life in freedom, what images do you see?"

Josef F nods. "They are colourful, vivid pictures. I sometimes see them in front of me before I fall asleep. Or after I wake up on the weekend, when I stay in bed a little longer. The amazed faces of the children, whose eyes reflect the light of star splashes on the Christmas tree. I see them trudging through the snow in a wildlife park, deer following us. We turn around to feed them with the corn grains we brought along. If I keep my eyes closed, I think I can smell the damp leaves. Or hear the birds chirping in the forest. I miss this here, in this world of concrete and steel. The only birds are the pigeons, whose cooing can be quite annoying. But I'm not complaining, because I've had a very nice, exciting life."

"And how do you cope with life in prison? I mean, how do you deal with having lost your freedom?" I ask further.

"You know, in the first few years it was very, very bad. It hurt a lot to have lost my freedom. Even as a child, I always loved my freedom and autonomy. I sometimes felt like an Indian. And then, when I lost my freedom, like a sad Indian. But I never gave up. I have learned to take things as they come. My life has never been easy, there were always obstacles in the way. And yet, I always took it with a sense of humour. I have mastered my entire life with this attitude. I'm not someone who lets things get him down. I want to grow old. But not in here!"

Amstetten in October 2022

I had to visit it. The place where Josef F spent his life, at least the majority of it. Also known as the scene of his crimes.

Amstetten is a tranquil district capital in the Mostviertel region. A typical piece of Lower Austria, not far from the border of Upper Austria. The cityscape seems small and orderly, with just over twenty thousand inhabitants living in buildings from different eras. Historic houses with several storeys line the shopping streets, with many buildings from the post-war period in between.

Josef F's former house is still standing. It found a new owner after a forced auction. As a first measure, he concreted over the cellar, then extensively renovated the house and created new flats. They are well rented, apparently the central location is appreciated.

The dark past of the house seems to have been buried with its cellar. I look at the old photos that still show it in its original state. Architecture is often an expression of the soul of the inhabitants, at least that's what architects say. The facade: grey, inconspicuous, unadorned. Boring, but also forbidding and cold. The interior is quite different; obstructed, entangled, separating the rooms instead of connecting them. In this way, it reflects the contradictory nature of Josef F as a person: outwardly unapproachable and cool, yet torn apart by conflicting, destructive forces on the inside.

***

I visit Josef F in prison in the afternoon. Once again, he seems introverted and thoughtful. "Even though everything happened so long ago, my wife is still inside me. More than before. I guess you get more sensitive with age. I think a lot about how she feels about everything now. It would be nice if she came to visit me. I think it's time to talk about what happened. To make a clean sweep, so to say. We have been married for sixty-nine years now, you can't just erase that!"

Josef F:

The life I was leading had long been exceeding my strength. I toyed with the idea of blowing the whistle and fleeing abroad to escape justice. I researched which countries had not concluded extradition agreements with Austria. I would have taken shelter there. I still had enough financial means to live on for a while. Nevertheless, it would not be easy. The whole world would see my act as a unique monstrosity of a beast. And what would become of my family? The media would hunt them down, perhaps the youth welfare office would take custody of my children? In the end, my whole family would fall into the abyss!

Those around me noticed my inner restlessness. I was hectic at work and was often told that I seemed absent-minded. My thoughts were constantly circling in search for a solution to the situation. But I could not find one.

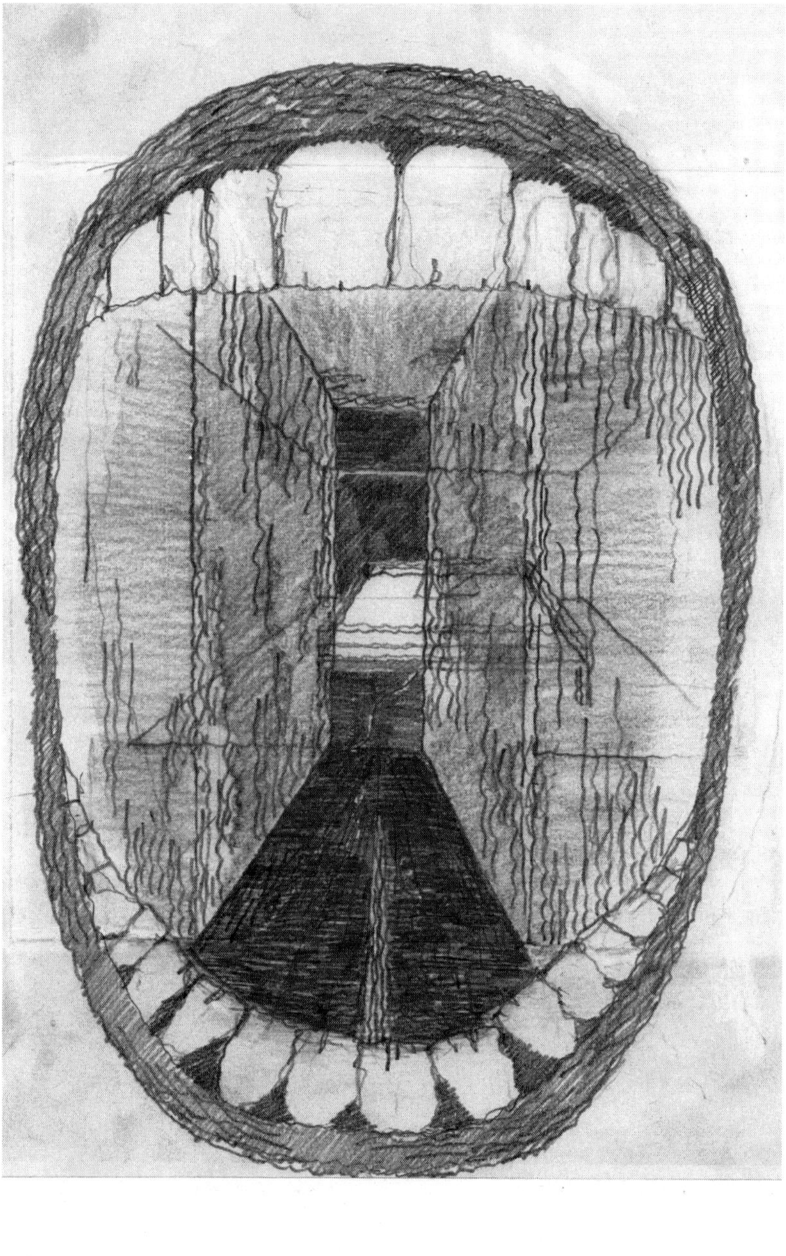

Stein Prison, interrogation zone, in October 2022

"Imagine what happened this week! They put such a little cart in front of my cell door. But not with me!" Josef F is indignant. His mischievous smile reveals that he is not taking it quite so seriously.

"A walker? Maybe just a precautionary measure of the judiciary," I remark.

"Yes, but not with me!" he repeats with a throwing away hand gesture and laughs. I have to agree with him. At almost ninety, Josef F is no longer the most agile, but he walks steadily and is generally in very good shape for his age. Perhaps thanks to his genes, but undoubtedly also due to the disciplined way he organises his daily life. He gets up at 5 a.m. sharp every day and does morning gymnastics. He puts a great deal of importance on staying physically fit. He also has, as he himself emphasises, a "healthy sleep". "Ever since I've been here, I haven't had a single sleepless night!" And he keeps a healthy diet. "Lots of vegetables, little meat. I grow tomatoes and peppers here in prison. Unfortunately, the lemons didn't turn out. Pastries, those are my weakness. I can't cook, but I can make an omelette. And apple strudel, pancakes, Kaiserschmarrn [14] or Buchteln [15]. All billions of calories, I know..." He laughs. "But I've kept my weight down, and that's not so easy here in prison!" Which he is right about.

---

[14] "Emperor's Mess", a lightly sweetened pancake that takes its name from the Austrian emperor (Kaiser) Franz Josef I

[15] oven-baked yeast dumplings, filled with either plum or apricot jam, and served with custard

You have to be disciplined in prison to avoid falling into a boring rut of doing nothing. They also cook very well and generously in the Stein Prison, as I know from other inmates. To keep himself mentally fit - "I know how important that is at my advanced age!" - Josef F is active as a writer. He is currently working on a manuscript about his life, from his childhood to education and to the remarkable professional career he has had.

"Stay healthy," I tell him as we say goodbye, and add with a wink: "By the way, I've now tried insects; crickets and mealworms. That's the food of the future, high in protein and very healthy!" He laughs and then bursts out: "In God's name, please no! I tried something like that in Thailand, that's not my thing. Even though I am otherwise open-minded when it comes to food. In Africa, I ate meat that was very tender. After asking, I found out that it was rat meat."

Josef F:

I had to devote myself to business tasks even during the Christmas holidays. It was the time to get paperwork done or draw sketches for a new, partially automated production plant. I often sat in the office until late in the evening. When the phone rang, I reluctantly picked it up. What customer was going to call now? When I heard her voice, my heart leapt: it was my young lover! But she sounded somehow troubled. "Do you have time to go out to dinner with me tonight? I'd love to see you again..." I immedia-

tely agreed, spurred on by the prospect of a little adventure with her. She suggested to choose the location and added, "We can also spend the night there, if you feel like it. I'm longing for you." Oh, how I felt like it! Her voice sounded seductive; I sensed her desire. I had experienced enough frustration lately, some variety in my sex life would do me good. And I longed for an intelligent conversation partner who might show me new ways of looking at things.

We agreed to meet at the train station. I watched her from a distance, apparently studying the timetable. A young man approached her. She dismissed him with a friendly smile. I had to smile on the inside. It filled me with pride that he apparently had no chance against me, the much older one. I stepped out of my cover and greeted her with a fleeting kiss on the cheek. I had to be careful, someone could see us. We got into my car which I had parked in front of the station and drove off. During the ride, she told me about the boring Christmas party at her house and that her family had now gone on a skiing holiday. She had chosen an elegant restaurant for us. We dined exquisitely and consumed quite a few drinks, which soon took effect. Of course, she had taken the precaution of reserving a double room. It was a night full of passion. She seemed to be completely sexually starved and I had trouble restraining her.

Stein Prison, interrogation zone, in November 2022

"Imagine who came here the other day! My wife! She was accompanied by her sister, that is, my sister-in-law. They were both wearing long dresses. They came to clean the windows and were standing on a ladder-"
"Excuse me?" I interject. "That's not possible, it's the housekeepers who clean here. You know that..."

"Yes, everyone keeps saying it was only a dream. But I am a down-to-earth person, not a dreamer! I really did see my wife in front of me! She smiled at me and said: 'Seppl, my family has now disowned me, too'. 'But why, you've always been there for everyone, you're a wonderful mother!' But she didn't say anything else, just smiled at me. I saw a sad glimmer in her eyes. That touched me so much, I've been thinking about it for days."
"Mr F, you definitely dreamt that," I clarify. "That's just how it is when you have internalised someone deeply. It can then happen that their image appears before you in a very real way, even if it is only a dream. But maybe it is also because something is gnawing at you. Your guilty conscience maybe?"[16]

And there it is again, that look from his bright eyes. Sad, helpless, almost desperate.

---

[16] *It is noted for clarification that Josef F's description of his wife's visit never took place. Indeed, it was a dream.*

Josef F:

During my holiday, a mountain of mail and call lists had accumulated that now had to be dealt with. First thing in the morning, my diligent secretary prepared a strong mocha for me. So strong, it could have brought the dead back to life! Then she let me know that some customers were waiting for me furiously, because their system had not been working for two weeks! I immediately rushed to my desk to call everyone back. It turned out to be a long day filled with phone calls and desk work. Tomorrow, I would have to visit numerous customers to deliver the required spare parts.

In the evening, I had gone out briefly to run a few errands for my trip. When I returned to my office, I was in for a surprise. My young lover had come! She was lounging lasciviously on the bed, leafing through a fashion magazine. When she heard me, she looked up seductively. I wasn't really in the mood for lovemaking, if only because of tomorrow's business trip. But she presented her figure again in her perky baby doll. A temptation that hardly any man could have resisted. I hurried to the bathroom right away to take a piece of Viagra. I took my time with the rest of the body care so that the pill could take effect. She never hesitated and was always quick to get to the point. When I returned to the bedroom, she had already taken off the baby doll. I couldn't be that tired not to get going right away. To be on the safe side, I set my alarm for 5 a.m. It would get late now and I desperately needed sleep, which I could hardly expect tonight.

The shrill ringing of the alarm clock startled me out of my deep sleep. I had to orient myself first. I rubbed the sleep out of my eyes and looked around. The side of the bed next to me was empty. I jumped up and ran into the kitchen. There I saw of my young lover, preparing breakfast for me.

***

The tour to the customers was very successful. The market situation was excellent at the time and many companies were expecting larger orders that they would not be able to handle with their current machinery. At least that took a little of the existential pressure off me that I was constantly under. There were nights when I woke up drenched in sweat and my existential fears prevented me from falling asleep again. Should I blow the whistle? But at what cost? As far as I was concerned, I would take responsibility of course, and go to prison. But the consequences would not only affect me, but my whole family! I tossed and turned restlessly in bed and imagined all kinds of horror scenarios. From today's point of view, it would probably have been wiser to give up and reveal the truth. But there is a difference between being in the middle of a tricky situation and judging it in retrospect.

Stein Prison, interrogation zone, in November 2022

"Looking back, do you think you had a good life?"

The answer comes quickly and decisively: "Yes, I had a good life. I enjoyed it. I loved the adventure, the risk, the danger! I had to conquer the mountains anywhere I went. I climbed Mount Kilimanjaro in Tanzania. It's a miracle I never crashed. Who knows, if I hadn't gone to prison, maybe I would have already fallen off a mountain by now." There it was again, his very special black humour. His talent for finding something positive in the worst of situations.

"I travelled the world when I was young," he continues. "My work at the steel company took me as far as Africa, where whole swathes of land were equipped with transmission masts: Ghana, South Africa, Namibia, Kenya. I have very many fond memories of that time. Africa has an unimagined vastness and depth. The colours are quite different there. Nature has its own sound, its own rhythm on this huge continent. I was able to experience wild animals in their natural habitat. I fed crocodiles, I loved playing with danger. I reached out very close, and not only once did one almost snap my hand. Once, a crocodile bit my finger. I can still see the orphaned lion cub we rescued. You must know that I am very fond of animals. People have tried to persuade me several times to try hunting, but I always refused. I could never shoot an animal, I'd drop the gun first! I love animals, I could never be cruel to them.

Yes, I have travelled a lot due to my work. I've been to India twice, for almost a year each time. The steel company I worked for had two big construction sites in the north of the country, in Rourkela and in Allahabad. From there, it's not far to the Himalayan mountains. With a few like-minded colleagues, I marched about four hundred metres up the southern slope of Mount Everest. India impressed me very much, I would like to go there again. Unfortunately, I don't know what has become of my offspring there..."

"You also have children in India?" I ask in amazement.

"Yes, three girls and two boys. Their mothers were very poor local women whom I gave a livelihood. I invested in a business, built a big tin hut where they could sell clothes."

I still can't believe what he is telling me. Are they even his children? No matter, the poor women with their children, they must have given him a lot. The feeling of taking responsibility seems to be particularly important to him.

"If you liked it so much, why did you leave the steel company?" I change the subject.

The answer I get again once again proves Josef F's contradictions: "This vagabond lifestyle couldn't go on like this. The months of being away, I had no time at all for my family! A marriage where one person is never at home can't work. So, I quit my job. Of course, I was never unemployed, I already had the next lucrative job in prospect. At a concrete company in my hometown. I became the boss of three hundred and fifty workers there."

"What would you do differently if you were young now and at the beginning of life?"

Josef F doesn't think long. "I always wanted a big family.

Because I always felt so terribly lonely as a child. But then, as a father, I probably did many things wrong. I was distant, stiff, almost cold. In reality, that came from my insecurity. I didn't know any better. My mother never had a thing for tenderness. Besides, I was hardly ever at home. Oh, I have done a lot of things wrong...".

"Let's leave the past, you can't change it anyway. How do you envisage your future life if you were released from prison?"

Josef F looks at me unconcerned. "I would move back to my hometown, I would find something there. I have achieved so much in life, I know I would also manage this new start. Believe it or not, I was a millionaire twice in my life before I lost everything again. I'm a stand-up guy, I've picked myself up every time."

I try to explain that he will probably get conditions and will be placed in an assisted living facility until further notice. He nods casually and doesn't seem particularly bothered.

"What do you miss most here in prison?"

"The relationship with my family. And the mountains! If I get the chance to leave prison, I will go to the mountains and go on a long hike. And I would travel, to Ghana, India, Luxembourg." Josef F pauses for a moment, as if reminiscing about the stages of his life, then continues. "But do you know where my very first path would take me?" "No, where to?" "My mother's grave," he enlightens me. "I have only just had the grave fees renewed again."

Josef F:

And another autumn rolled in. Most of the orders were delivered especially in the months of September and October, and I had to be on site with many customers during the assembly. In mid-November, the electronics unexpectedly failed on a large concrete pipe production machine in southern Styria. The customer sounded completely desperate on the phone, so I had no choice but to go there immediately. I knew him to be difficult and vindictive, I couldn't afford to get on his bad side.

When I arrived in southern Styria, the owner was already running towards me, panting. He described the technical problem to me on the way to the plant. He had accepted a large order and had now run into delivery difficulties due to the breakdown, and was already threatened with the withdrawal of the order. After a test run, I was quickly able to determine where the electronic fault lay. Fortunately, I had already guessed it beforehand and had the right replacement part with me, so the problem was quickly solved. The owner thanked me profusely and filled my boot to the brim with cases of the best Styrian wine. I had to decline his invitation to stay for dinner though, because I wanted to get home as soon as possible.

During the drive through mountainous landscapes, a bad premonition came over me. It was gradually getting dark outside, and the thoughts inside me were getting darker, too. An anxious feeling came over me, which was increasing to the point that I panicked. As I sped along the motorway, getting closer and closer to my destination, I felt my heart pounding wildly.

Stein Prison, interrogation zone, in November 2022

Josef F often describes the events in his manuscript differently than what the court later based his conviction on. According to him, he should not be considered a criminal. Especially not a murderer. I'm interested to know why he then immediately accepted the sentence, even the guilty verdict for murder. "Because I still feel guilty. I should have ended the situation. But I was too weak. Yes, I feel guilty. That's why I accepted the sentence as the court had decided." He looks straight at me, with his bright eyes. Today they seem dull, lifeless, sad. Is it because of the bluish shadows, the furrows that appear deeper than usual? I have the impression that his sadness is real.

It had been raining heavily that morning, but by the time I leave the prison, the clouds have cleared. I drive through the beautiful landscape of the Wachau, its late autumn colours are shining in the sunlight. But my thoughts revolve around darker topics. The conversation we had earlier still has its effect on me. As a criminal defence lawyer, one is constantly confronted with images of murder victims. The expression on their faces is often gruesome and gives an idea of the horror of the last seconds of their lives, sometimes appearing stunned, as if death had taken them by surprise. One becomes hardened and after some time, flips through the files emotionlessly, in order to highlight important passages with a marker or to make notes for the defence strategy. It is different when it comes to children. The sight of the small, bluish discoloured, bent bodies does not let go so quickly.

They reveal the apparent meaninglessness of our existence. It is hard to bear when little people die, even though they have not yet begun to really live.

Josef F:

I went to my office around 10 p.m., checked the requests, signed everything as prepared by my secretary and took care of the mail. The envelope was the last one in the pile, with no return address on it. It just said "For Josef - private". I opened it and started reading. "I long for you..." I was overcome with melancholy. I, too, was longing for my young lover. But at the moment, I was once again plagued by dark thoughts that thoroughly spoiled my desire for love and passion. They revolved around my dark secret, which had stayed undiscovered for decades now. Where would all of this lead? How to get out of it without causing more damage? For the first time in my life, I was really lost. The oppressive feeling of not being able to find a way out almost drove me mad.

The job I had also entailed a great deal of responsibility. It required deliberate action with a cool head, because improper troubleshooting could lead to life-threatening hazardous situations. In retrospect, I was very lucky that nothing happened despite my burdensome private situation.

***

Suddenly I thought I had found the solution to my problem: I had to set myself a deadline. A date when I would dissolve the existing situation. No matter what would come after that! I had always been a person who stood by his responsibilities. I had not been afraid to make important decisions. And now I had to make a decision of great consequence: My double life had to come to an end once and for all.

Stein Prison, interrogation zone, in November 2022

"You told me that your mother was very religious and took you to church every Sunday. And I read that religious rites like baptism have always meant something to you. Are you a believer?"

Josef F clears his throat before showing me his left thumb. I notice a small injury at the tip where the nail bends a little.

"This reminds me of an experience I will never forget. I was sixteen and an apprentice. The master assigned me to wind copper wires. My hand slipped and my thumb got caught in the machine. It was crushed so deeply that I almost lost consciousness and had to be taken to the emergency hospital. There, I was anaesthetised with ether, as was customary at the time. I still remember the image of a huge, colourful tunnel that led to a funnel-shaped exit. Everything was filled with harmonious sounds. Astonished by all the splendour, I stopped. In the same moment, I felt someone strike my cheeks and woke up. I looked into the face of the nurse. She looked relieved. 'Thank God you're back, I've been patting your face left and right. I was afraid you wouldn't wake up!' Who knows where my path would have led me if I hadn't stopped in that tunnel. But I guess there were still tasks waiting for me in this world."

"So, you believe in a supernatural power?"

"There must be. There must have been something like an initial spark for our existence. Basically, everything is connected to electrical engineering."

"What do you think is the meaning of life?"

"Making the most of it. Being active as long as you can. I have always lived very much for my work. The many trips abroad and the technical challenges on the construction sites have filled my life. And now, in prison, I try to stay fit, because I definitely don't want to become bedridden. That's the annoying thing about getting old, the muscle strength decreases… But I still feel as fit as a fiddle! You know that I would love to build another house? I realise that it's probably not going to happen anymore. But in any case, I want to go hiking again when I get the chance. I want to build up my body again slowly, and then also tackle further, difficult routes."

"That means you still have dreams?"

"Definitely, I still have dreams for the future. And many plans for the rest of my life. I have also already imagined what the day of my release would be like. The first thing I would do is treat myself to a cold beer!"

In a wildlife park in November 2022

I happen to be in the area and spontaneously decide to set off here for a solitary hike. In his manuscript, I read that Josef F liked to go on excursions to wildlife parks, so he must have been to this one, too.

I can feel the chilly late autumn weather. The leaves rustle under my steps. I leave the stress of everyday life behind me and pause briefly to breathe in the fresh, damp air of the forest. The sky above me is cloudy, almost magically shimmering in various shades of grey. As I close my eyes, I see images of my dream from last night. At first only dimly, then becoming clearer. Mysterious clouds of mist lie over the forest floor. The bare branches draw sharp, grotesque contours. The atmosphere is of peculiar silence. No birdsong, no sounds of nature.

Dawn starts to set in. I quicken my steps to reach the car park before nightfall. But this forest seems to have no end. The path narrows visibly, finally disappearing into an almost impenetrable thicket. The realisation comes like a silent companion of which you suddenly become aware, although he has always been walking beside you: something evil is lurking in this place. A breath of ice-cold air brushes my cheek, creeps into my body, like a harbinger of approaching disaster. Now it is almost pitch dark around me, the trees only black shadows. There, they seem to be moving, coming menacingly towards me! Loud, cracking breaks through the night. Suddenly, the ground beneath me gives way to my step, I fall into a deep pit. A trap! Someone has dug a deep hole in the ground and covered it up with branches.

I don't remember how the dream ended. I must have woken up. Lost in thought, I stroll on, trying to get to the bottom of myself. The association with what is currently occupying me is obvious. What is it that makes me so interested in this story that it even haunts me in my dreams? Is it this conglomerate of the most diverse traits that characterise the main protagonist? Josef F was unbridled and obsessed with power. Immovable in his attitudes. Relentless. Unbending. Indestructible. Perhaps something about him reminds me of the "wild grandfathers" in my own family? One of my great-grandfathers, as I know from my grandmother's stories, was a rafter in the Drau Valley in Carinthia. A physically extremely hard job, often involving danger to life when getting the felled wood driven downstream. This great-grandfather is said to have been a "wild dog", and on top of that a so called "manwhore". When he passed away, the priest at the funeral kept on lamenting about his immoral lifestyle. Until the daughter of the deceased stood up and exclaimed: "That's enough scolding now, Father. Now it's time to bury 'im!" I still smile today when I think of this family anecdote. I was often admonished when I was young. "Where is your respect for authority?"

Maybe I have something in my genes from that ancestor who put the priest in his place. Perhaps it lies in our family, this unyieldingness towards the authority. I have kept it until today, even if it gets me into trouble again and again. In the end, I have learned that you can only reach your goals through perseverance. Respect from judges or colleagues can only be gained through straightforwardness and performance, never through pitiful attempts at ingratiation. Admittedly, this key to success demands a lot of diligence, commitment and discipline.

Qualities that one certainly cannot deny Josef F.

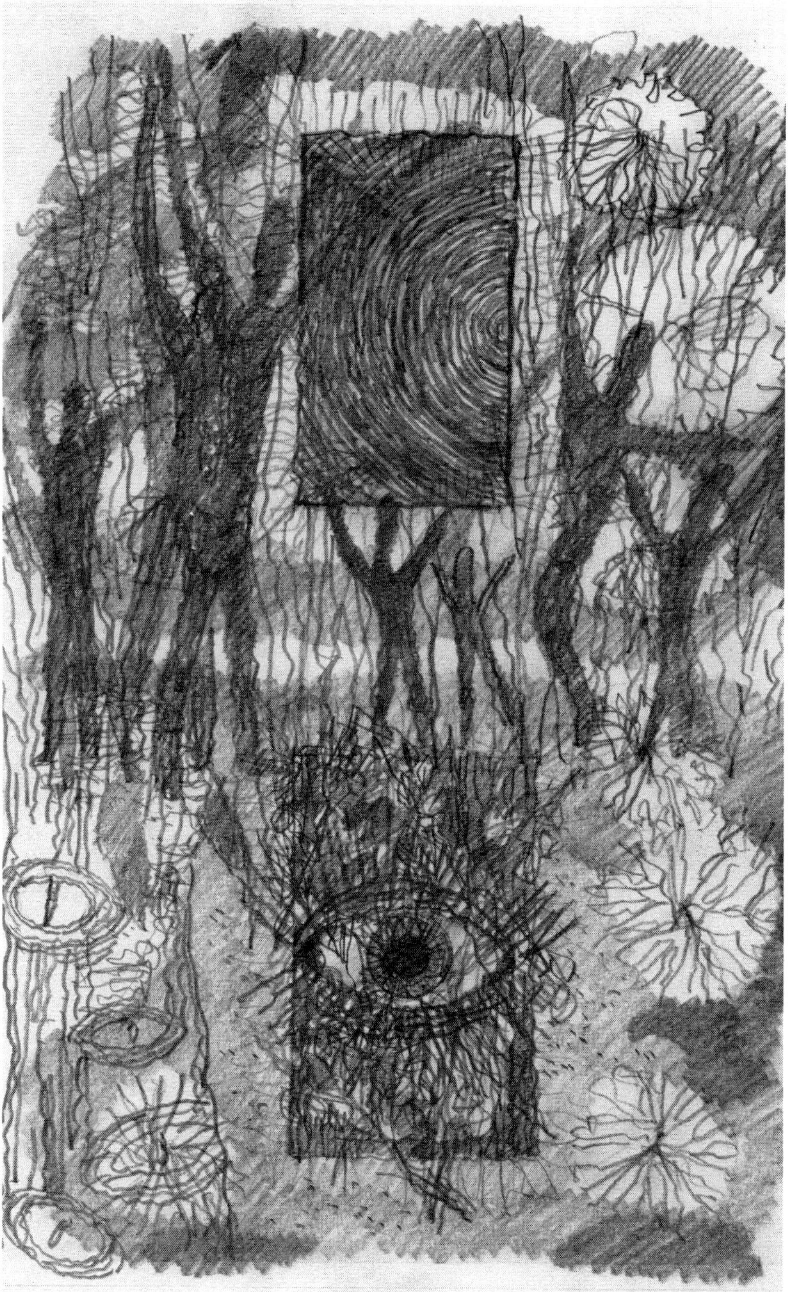

Josef F:

In the following years, I acquired several properties, including a large apartment building with 22 flats and a shop on the ground floor. With that I burdened myself with quite some expenses, as the acquisition naturally required a lot of repairs and renovations. Fortunately, my investments in securities also continued to grow. My economic situation had become so stable that at least the financial pressure had ceased. All these were good conditions for my planned exit from the double life.

Stein Prison, interrogation zone, in November 2022

"It is known that inmates convicted of sexual offences are often attacked by fellow inmates. Has this happened to you, too?"

"Yes. It was in the infirmary. I was there for a blood test. Suddenly, the man behind me hit me started hitting me hard in the back of my neck at rapid intervals. The officer just watched. I turned to the side, but kept standing. I have my pride, after all. He was a big, strong man, a Chechen. I didn't report him. I don't want any trouble, just my peace. Of course, I learned how things work here in prison, to avoid getting into trouble. I was still a newcomer and I was at the ZKM when a scuffle suddenly broke out between several people. I was still quite well-trained at the time and tried to intervene. The officer immediately stepped in and told me to never do that again."

To explain: "ZKM" is the German abbreviation for "Central Clothes Magazine" at Stein Prison. In this area, the inmates' personal belongings are stored, for example clothes or cash, which is why it is also called the "deposit station". It is not generally accessible to inmates. If a prisoner wants to store or retrieve something from there, he must first submit a corresponding request to the prison management.

A few days later, I happen to meet my former client Wilfried W, who was an inmate at Stein Prison until 2012. I ask him about Josef F. "As a normal inmate, you had almost no access to him," he explains to me. "I saw him a few times from the window in the yard. He did his rounds there alone, accompanied only by three prison guards. He has been put under special surveillance for his own safety, wherever he went in prison. Even just to take a shower. There was quite a commotion when he arrived in Stein. His case also caused waves among us prisoners, and there were some who whispered to each other: 'If I meet the cellar monster, I'll break all his bones!'"

Josef F:

In the meantime, spring had once again arrived. My ever-so-reliable secretary had recently resigned because she had been offered a crisis-proof job as a civil servant. I didn't like that at all, but I had to bite the bullet. On the other hand, I was already over sixty and thinking of cutting back a bit. Everyone welcomed this decision. At last, I would have more time for the family. And for myself, I hoped. I took part in mountain hikes and small climbing tours again, went on excursions with the children and visited fairs with them. To everyone's delight, I made a plan to build a big swimming pool in the garden. "You are much more balanced now," I was praised. And, "old age has obviously made you content and happy!" How clueless they were.

Stein Prison, interrogation zone, in November 2022

Josef F disagrees with much of what the media has reported about him. In some respects, he is even right. The media copy each other's reports, creating legends that are spread without being verified. Some people refer to the "post-factual age", in which the focus is no longer on the truth, but on the impact of a news story on the media consumer. Media diversity is a good thing, but one must also be able to handle it by not believing everything that is published. This applies, for example, to the completely unfounded rumour that Josef F had also locked up his own elderly mother for years until her death.

Nevertheless, I do not have the impression that Josef F would suffer particularly from his public condemnation of "the cellar monster". He seems to have settled in at Stein Prison, where he was sent after his conviction and where he has been living for many years now. He gets along well with the officials. Everyone is friendly, he is a "popular inmate". "I am nice and polite to everyone, and that is appreciated."

I am interested in whether his attitude towards criminals has changed since he has been in prison. For example, towards murderers.

"There are many people in here who have killed-" I begin my sentence.

"Unimaginable for me!" he interrupts me. "I could never kill anyone. Especially not my own flesh and blood."

No, Josef F does not want to be put on the same level as murderers and killers.

***

The next day, I visit a client in the Vienna-Josefstadt Prison. He had strangled his wife with his bare hands and is charged with murder. She had cancer in a hopeless stage. He wanted to give her a dignified existence until the end. Until he couldn't stand the pressure, the pain and suffering anymore and let himself be carried away to commit the unimaginable. I will be defending him in court in the near future, and I have already made notes for my opening statement. It will begin with the words "Life has many more facets than there can be paragraphs." A wise sentence, which I have also put on my homepage. As a criminal defence lawyer, you are confronted again and again with cases that challenge long-established views and entrenched positions. You learn to look beyond the "legal horizon".

No, you are not necessarily a bad person if you have killed. Just as you're not automatically a good person just because you get through life with no criminal record.

Josef F:

In the following summer, my new swimming pool in the garden was finally completed. The pool measured eight by four metres and was 1.7 metres deep. It had a movable roof with attached showers, toilets and changing rooms. It looked fantastic. I organised a big inauguration party with many guests and their children. A radiant celebration with sunshine and cloudless sky. I had ordered delicious ice-cream specialities, which were in high demand. The guests frolicked enthusiastically in the large swimming pool, the water almost overflowed, and the garden was also almost too small for the many happily laughing people.

In my law office in November 2022

Children. I read about them again and again in his manuscript. How they run towards him joyfully, how he takes them in his arms and lifts them up. How they tease him with their games. How they hide from him and there is a big laugh when he finds them. How he hides eggs and chocolate bunnies in nests at Easter. "Every time they found a nest, there was a delighted cry! I couldn't get enough of the sight of their happy faces." About the moment when he let a blue budgie flutter out of its cage. "Their mouths dropped open in amazement, and I knew that I had chosen the right present." About the shining eyes of the children in front of the Christmas tree. Images that are in no way compatible with the terrible events. Yet, they show that Josef F also had longings for harmony, peace and love. But his negative personality traits, above all his disastrous delusion of control, were overpowering and determined his path in life, with all the devastating consequences.

Josef F:

And once again, autumn has come into the country. A season that also brings all kinds of work in and around the house with it. We had a small pond, where colourful iridescent goldfish were swimming around. I now had to catch them, pump out the water and then clean the bottom of the pond. The mud was used to water our currant, raspberry and blackberry bushes. Then, the water lilies had to be trimmed. When everything was cleaned up, I refilled the pond with water and let the fish back in.

And so my life went on in a quiet way. A deceptive calm, as it would soon turn out.

Stein Prison, interrogation zone, in November 2022

Josef F is sitting in front of me today in a tracksuit with his shoulders hunched up. He seems gloomy. "I had a terrible nightmare. I was in bed, in a room that looked almost exactly like my cell. But only almost. There were little details that made me realise I'm somewhere else. The coffee machine was a different colour and smaller. The wall calendar was hanging upside down. The things on the desk were arranged differently. It was as if someone had deliberately recreated everything, but had made little mistakes. As if there was an evil, cunning plan behind it. The thought of what they wanted to do to me crept into my head. Panic started to overcome me..."

He is so upset that I am really worried. "Please look after yourself," I tell him. "You are so good at expressing yourself. Write about what's troubling you. Write it off your chest."

He looks at me for a long time, very seriously.

"What incident in your life touched you the most?" I ask into his silence.

"Something that happened after I was already in prison. It was the death of my adult son. He looked like me, but only on the outside. He was tall and handsome. But he was sensitive. When my crimes were uncovered, he must have taken it very much to heart. One day, I found out that he had passed away. He was only thirty-five. It still hurts so much, I can't even talk about it..." His voice fails. The slight twitch in his eyes reveals how agitated he is.

"We all have wounds on our souls," I finally say. "It's not easy to look into them. But it's good to talk them off your chest."

I would have liked to talk longer with Josef. F that morning. He seemed different than usual. For the first time, I felt it: The wounded soul hidden deep inside him.

In my law office in November 2022

It is Friday afternoon, when once again a number with a Graz area code appears on the display of my mobile phone. It is my former client Alfred U: "I have to tell you something you should know. They led Josef F in a wheelchair past my cell to the infirmary today. Unfortunately, I don't know any details!"

Sick inmates are treated on an outpatient basis in the infirmary wing of Stein Prison or, if necessary, admitted as inpatients. The specialists work there on a daily basis, but no major operations are performed. If an operation is required, the inmate is transferred to the nearby regional hospital Landesklinikum Krems, where he is accommodated in the closed ward, the prison hospital. I hope this will not be necessary for Josef F!

While I am still thinking about this, Mr U has long since moved on to another topic. He expresses his displeasure about a lurid television report about his own case, which apparently flickered across the screens a few weeks ago. "'Sex sells', you know that," I remark placatingly and thank him for the important information regarding Josef F.

Stein Prison, interrogation zone, in November 2022

Josef F looks well on this Thursday morning and is in good spirits. "I felt a bit unwell and unsteady on my feet. They put me through my paces for three days in the infirmary. I was certified to be in the best of health. But I really need to drink more..."

"Water, of course," I interject with a grin.

He laughs. "There's no alcohol here anyway!"

Then he goes on to tell me about his stay in the infirmary. "One of the prison guards on duty there has the same surname as a dear resident of our house back from when I was a child. I took that as a good omen, because Mitzi saved my life three times back then."

"How?"

"The first time I was four and swimming in a big pool, when a Russian soldier threw a hand grenade into it! Mitzi immediately jumped into the water, grabbed me and pulled me out, and just then the grenade exploded.
A few weeks later, I almost died again. I was lying on the floor, screaming and writhing in pain. Mitzi came running

into our flat, terrified. She took me to the hospital, where they pumped out my stomach. Food poisoning! You know, we had to save money, so my mum and I ate nothing but sausages the whole week. When the supply ran out, some of them were already mouldy...

Well, and then Mitzi saved my life once again. I was already seven and suddenly got a high fever. My mum didn't take it too seriously. Mitzi made sure that I got to the hospital in time. They diagnosed a foreskin contraction there. I had surgery right away."

"They say you once saved a woman's life, too," I point out. I had read about it somewhere and had actually wanted to ask him about it for a long time.

"That's right. It was in Amstetten. I saw pitch-black smoke pouring out of a window and immediately went in with a neighbour. The woman was lying lifeless on the floor with a burning ironing board next to her! We pulled her out quickly and I immediately started mouth-to-mouth resuscitation. She survived. But I was quite disgusted, because she smelled so strongly of alcohol..."

Josef F:

In August 2006, the media were suddenly full of headlines about a young girl who had escaped from the house of her kidnapper in a small town in Lower Austria, where she had been held captive for eight years. Considering my own situation, the events touched me. I began to think more and more about possible exit scenarios. I kept reassuring myself: When the time came, I would find a good defence lawyer and surely get off with a lenient sentence.

Stein Prison, interrogation zone, in November 2022

The famous kidnapping case of Natascha Kampusch was uncovered around two years before the arrest of Josef F. Wolfgang Priklopil had kidnapped a girl just six years old, and wanted to mould her into his "dream woman"; a submissive partner who would read his every wish from his eyes. I decide to ask Josef F about the case.

"What do you think of Natascha Kampusch?"

His eyes flash. "A great woman! What she's been through, and yet he hasn't been able to break her. Respect. It's shameful how hostile some people in this country are to her."

"Did you follow the events back then?"

"Yes, of course, it was a huge case. Newspapers, television, everything was full of it. Of course, it made me think about my own situation. But I always knew that I would never kill myself, like Kampusch's abductor did. I cherish life too much for that. God will know when my time has come."

Josef F:

Winter arrived with icy coldness. Because of my newfound free time, I had devoted more time to winter sports like skiing, ice skating and tobogganing. I love winter because it transforms the forest surroundings around my hometown into a magical world of ice and snow. A new feeling of melancholy took hold of me more and more. I felt that all the things I was now experiencing had an expiry date. The end of my double life was coming closer and closer. There would be criminal consequences for me. I would go to prison, there was no doubt about that. I brooded a lot and ate up my worries inside myself. Far and wide there was no one I could confide in.

Stein Prison, interrogation zone, in December 2022

He greets me in his usual friendly manner, but today he seems in a particularly good mood. He is wearing a cream-colored woollen pullover. After all, it is already November. After we sit down, he fixes me with his alert, light grey eyes and begins to speak.

"That dream came back. I was told that it could only be a dream. But it all felt so real! It was night, and suddenly I woke up. I was lying in bed and looked at the clock, it showed half past eight. I looked around and realised that I wasn't in my own cell. But in some kind of cell-like construction! It looked deceptively similar to my own cell, but with small deviations. And then it began. The walls went up, and a huge, unique, colourful show unfolded around me. Suddenly, the pop singer Roland Kaiser appeared and raised his powerful, masculine voice. It was all about me, about my case, he was basically processing it vocally! It was like a musical! A few young people were looking inside through a side window. A woman pointed at me and said, 'he doesn't look so bad'. 'Dirnderl [17], you don't need to be afraid of me,' I answered and laughed. Roland Kaiser's voice filled the room, it was very impressive. The whole spectacle lasted until two in the morning. I could have got up and fled at any time. In between, I called out to the night watchman 'I feel endangered here!' But nobody came."

---

[17] *In Bavarian (and other German) dialects, "Dirnderl" or "Dirndl" meant "young woman".*

"I'm sure it was a very strange dream. Maybe you fell asleep watching TV while the programme 'Schlagerkarussell'[18] was on? Maybe that's how you process your experiences? Don't you think you've been scarred by the way you've lived? The double life for decades, then the media spectacle, the sensational trial... You can't just put that away."

Josef F waves it off. "Well, the psychiatrists have diagnosed me with all kinds of things. They'll know. I think it's good that I'm getting therapy here. But you know, I have a suspicion: They want to make a film about me and my life in here!"

Josef F:

I felt that it would be my last New Year's Eve in freedom. The people around me seemed relaxed and happy. I politely listened to their stories. In my mind, I was completely elsewhere, though. I kept my New Year's resolutions to myself: to visit people who are important to me one last time. Settle my personal and business affairs. Leave my will with the notary.

In the following months, I retreated to solitary hikes in the woods. No one suspected what was going on inside me. They would find out soon enough.

---

[18] *a hit carousel, a TV programme with pop music and oldies*

In my law office in December 2022

I finished reading the manuscript today. I put the folder aside and close my eyes. Thoughts and images flood my brain. The few people involved in my project, who know I am writing a book about this case, have asked me: "It is one of the most horrific crimes of the century. What does that do to you?"

As a criminal defence lawyer, I have been used to looking into abysses for decades. However, there is something about this abyss that won't let me go. A gloomy, shall room appears in my mind. It smells of mould. I can't breathe. I continue to walk through narrow corridors. What was that? I pause for a moment to locate the soft, scraping sound. There, a small shadow in a corner, something black darts out and disappears just as quickly. A rat? I can't see anything in the semi-darkness. I quickly walk on. The oppressive feeling gets stronger, panic spreads through me: Is there an end to this narrow passage? At the same moment, I feel the door cleverly hidden behind an open shelf. I run to it and shake it violently. Boards fall crashing to the floor. Suddenly, it bursts open. I see a spiral staircase in front of me and, at the top, a bright slit from which daylight seems to emerge. I rush up the steps, it gets brighter. Once again, I am standing in front of a wooden door. I push against it until it creaks open. Now I am in a large garden. Birds are chirping. I feel the fresh breeze on my skin, turn my face into the warming sun, breathe in the scent of grass and trees. It's all so intense, as if I had spent decades in a cellar and had come back to life in just that moment.

"Beep-beep". My mobile phone beep has woken me up. I glance at the display. I had only dozed off for a few minutes, but the dream images have captivated me with their incomparable power.[19]

Josef F:

If I had wanted to, I could have fled any time this last week. There was enough money that I could have withdrawn. I also knew someone abroad where I could go into hiding. But I also wanted to stand by my responsibility, even in this situation. I didn't want to sneak away cowardly, because after all, I was responsible for this whole disaster.

I felt it would be goodbye forever and whispered, "Farewell, and never stop fighting. Life is worth living." As the sliding door opened to the outside, I caught sight of the criminal police officers positioned behind the pillars of the hall. We were surrounded by them immediately. They pulled me aside and one of them showed me his badge.

I wanted to get it over with quickly and urged them to proceed. The handcuffs clicked. It was over.

The interrogation began with the standard phrases. "You have the right to remain silent and the right to an attorney."

---

[19] *It is explicitly emphasised that this was a dream, without reference to any real place.*

Stein Prison, interrogation zone, in December 2022

"Do you still remember your arrest?" I ask Josef F.

"You bet. The officers interrogated me for hours. After two days, I was transferred from the police station to the regional court. Or rather smuggled! Looking out of the car, I saw a meadow that was not green, but black. Covered with reporters! They followed us everywhere with their cameras.

And then there was the trial itself: What a huge fuss! The car of the judicial guard I was in had to drive around the courthouse a few times, because the whole place was blocked by the reporters' vehicles. I am still grateful to the officers that they protected me so well back then. They formed a real chain around me, so that no one could get through."

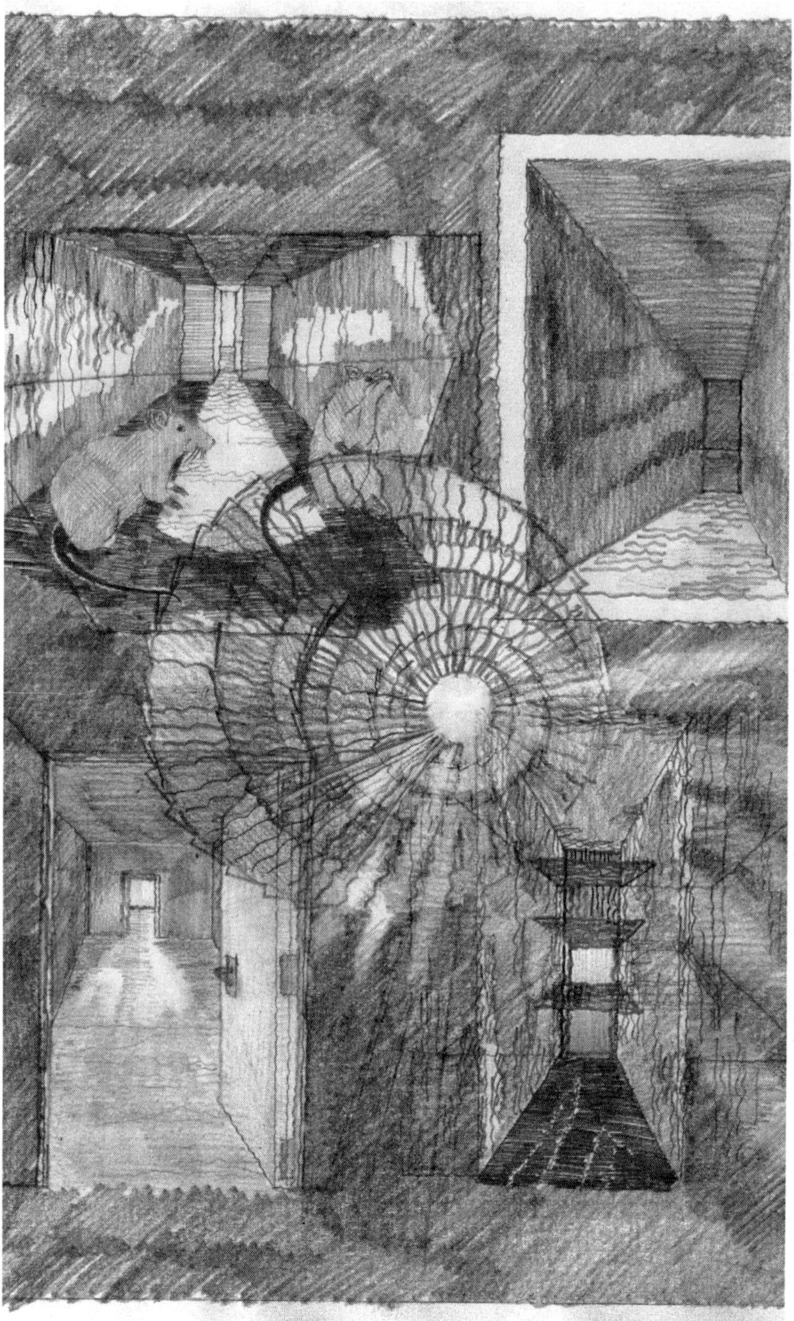

Josef F:

By far not everything happened as it was portrayed by the media. They made millions with my story, yet smeared me with dirt. But although I was labelled the "cellar monster", there were people who did not let themselves be deterred. I received hundreds of letters from all over the world, in which I was encouraged and offered support.

Stein Prison, interrogation zone, in December 2022

"It is often stated in the media that you get so much fan mail. Especially from women. Is that true?"

"Yes, loads of it! Especially in the beginning. All the letters are now stored in the depot, they weren't even given to me anymore. A woman from Upper Austria wrote to me for a long time. She lived near where my eldest daughter lived. I got lots of love letters from her, with lines like 'I kiss you every day' and so on. She told me about her difficult life, which was probably marked by many strokes of fate. She said that she was good at empathising with other people. Even someone like me. Then I ended it."

"Why is that?"

"Just because of her handwriting I had to! It was so 'schiach'[20] that sometimes I couldn't even decipher it. And at some point, her expressions of love became too much for me. I wrote her a goodbye letter: 'Let's leave it be. I may never get out of prison again. One day, I would only be a burden to you.' You know, I don't want a relationship at my age anymore. Besides, I am still married to my wife. If I were released, I would like to be with her again. Live with her in a house, even with separate bedrooms. Of course, only if she still wants that, if she still believes in me. In any case, I am always here for her. I would be really pleased if you got in touch with her. As you can see, I am a loyal dog."

"As you know, this has been portrayed quite differently in public. For example, there is a video circulating on the internet that a friend of yours supposedly made. Apparently, you were in Thailand with him. The images suggest that it was a sex holiday."

"Nonsense. It was a normal holiday. I never went to prostitutes," Josef F clarifies with a dismissive wave of his hand. "The friend is from Munich and was a regular guest at my campsite at Lake Mondsee. There were actually three of us. His stepfather was there, too."

"And why didn't your wife come along?"

"Oh, my wife couldn't stand the heat!"

"Doesn't it hurt that you have no contact with your family?" I inquire.

---

[20] *a colloquial Viennese expression, in this case meaning illegible and ugly handwriting*

He seems to face the unchangeable with equanimity. "I leave it up to them. If they want to get in touch with me, they will. I don't want to impose myself on them. I just want them to be safe financially. That's why I came up with the idea of a book. I like your cover suggestion!"

A few weeks ago, I had already shown him a painting by the Viennese painter Gerhard Häupler, who had portrayed him years ago as part of a series on notorious offenders. He had only glanced at the small colour print. I'm surprised he even remembers the picture.

"Once I am gone, my family will hopefully benefit from the royalties and will be able to build a house," he says.

Before I say goodbye to him, I have one more question for him: "Do you know what surprises me? That you still remember so many details. Even the Kaiserschmarrn..."

"She made the best Kaiserschmarrn in the world!" he clarifies with a smile. And adds, "You know, right after my conviction, when I came here to Stein, I started writing down my memories. I did a kind of life balance. At that time, I still remembered many events well. In the years that followed, I revised what I had written. And, of course, I changed it to the extent that no one would recognise him or herself. I used other names, but also altered the sequence of events. I don't want to embarrass anyone. Especially not the women I loved".

***

On the ride home, the raspy voice of Dan McCafferty fills the air from the car radio. The lead singer of the hard rock group "Nazareth" passed away just a few weeks ago.

"Dream on, though it's hard to tell, though you're foolin' yourself, dream on...". I love this song and turn up the volume to the max. Its fragile, yet powerful sound seems to fit in with the thoughts that I am having right now. Of the force of fate that shapes people and their paths. Of the longing that hides behind hard masks. Of Josef F's life, which was full of secret desires, power fantasies, lies, and shattered dreams. Now that I have processed his manuscript and had many conversations with him, I can sense the deep inner turmoil of this person. I have come closer to the incomprehensible things that drove him to his acts, without really being able to understand them. Many of the things he wrote or said are difficult or impossible to reconcile with the reality of the terrible events. Is he really the "emotionally illiterate" that the psychiatric expert described at the trial? Incapable of perceiving the feelings of others, let alone understanding them? In the last few months, I have come to know Josef F as a multi-layered, intelligent person who can also laugh at himself. The bizarre, paranoid dreams he has told me about are probably the expression of unconscious fears that inevitably had to develop under the enormous pressure of his decades-long double life. He seems to actually believe the pictures are real, even though he smiled at my remark that he must have fallen asleep during the TV programme "Schlagerkarussell". Josef F is now 87 years old and has become a little whimsical, but there is no sign of worrying dementia in him. He has retained his quick wit. Sometimes his mischievous nature flashes through. And he still has a good short-term memory.

But there is also his other, dark side. I know that he had already been sentenced in 1969, to an unconditional prison term of 18 months for "aggravated sexual abuse" of a woman. When I asked him about it, he dodged the question. He told me about misunderstandings and how it is when men misinterpreted signals from women.

Weeks later, he came back to the subject on his own. "It would have been good if I'd received therapy after the first time!"

"You mean after your first conviction?"

"Yes. I made a terrible mistake. I can still see her. She was standing at the window, sparsely dressed, waving at her boyfriend. At that moment, something flashed inside me... I served my sentence until the last day. But I didn't get any therapy! And that would have been important, especially because I was a first-time offender. After I was released, I dived into work, started a big family and bought several properties. I was successful and respected. There was no time left for reflection... I didn't look at my problems."

Is he reflecting now? "Looking" at his problem? Certainly, he was and is encouraged to do so within the framework of the therapies he has already received. And yet, I have the impression that his situation is no different from that of many people who have committed serious crimes: They are often unable to grasp the true depth of their guilt. They have carved out their own truth in order not to be crushed by their guilt.

Stein Prison, interrogation zone, in December 2022

Christmas is two weeks away. Yesterday, the client who strangled his terminally ill wife was acquitted of murder and sentenced to seven years in prison for manslaughter instead. I am relieved.

Today, I want to visit Josef F to wish him a Merry Christmas and a Happy New Year. It is somehow fitting, after having spent so much time together this year. He is already sitting in the interrogation room and smiles kindly when he sees me coming.

Again, I notice how unusually bright his eyes are. Maybe it's because of the bright red training jacket he is wearing today. "Red is my favourite colour," he informs me when I ask. But it's not so important what you wear in here," and adds mischievously, "unless you have visitors."

"How are you going to spend the holidays?" I ask.

"Christmas stopped existing for me a long time ago. In here, it's a day like any other," he explains, a little dully.

"No Christmas decorations in the cell at all?"

"Just a bit of fir brushwood. Because it smells so nice..."

"Do the inmates get anything special to eat on Christmas Eve?"

"I guess there will be a biscuit roulade again, like last year. Or chocolate cookies," he explains with a smile. "But I have to hold myself back, because of my figure!"

I notice the walker parked behind the glass wall. "Oh, I don't really need it. But the doctor, she insists on it, and it's better not to argue with a woman," he remarks with a wink, and then adds: "Sometimes, it's fun for me to run away from the officers with the walker. They often can't keep up with me!"

***

"I will coerce Mr Josef F to a Christmas menu," Alfred U declares with a touch of irony. I visited him afterwards to also wish him a Merry Christmas. "We will have baked pangasius with fake vegetable mayonnaise. It's made of yoghurt, mustard and sour cream. Tastes much better and is healthier than real mayonnaise." I can't help but feel happy, knowing there is someone who cares about someone like Josef F.

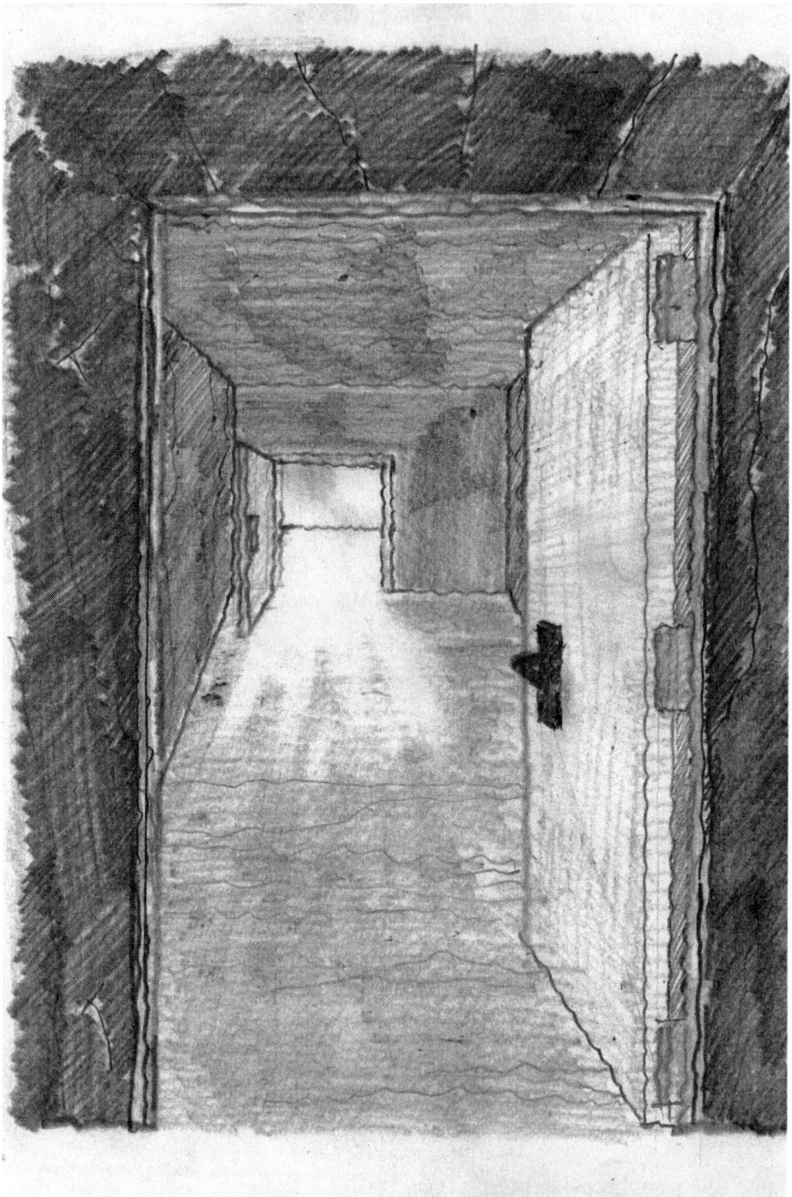

Addendum: Immovable

After fifteen years, a prisoner sentenced to life imprisonment is entitled by law the possibility of being released on parole. Josef F must not be denied this right, either. However, it is not quite so simple in his case; he is still in the special prison unit for the criminally insane.

According to the law, the aim of this enforcement is to treat the mentally abnormal inmate. A release can only be considered when a corresponding "reduction of dangerousness", as it is called in psychiatric jargon, has taken place. The court must therefore obtain a psychiatric report at regular intervals, but at least every two years, to see whether the mental abnormality still exists or whether a corresponding reduction in dangerousness has occurred.

The expert in psychiatry and neurology Dr Wolfgang Soukoup last examined Josef F in April 2021. In his expert reports of August 17th, and August 24th, 2021, he concluded that that the severe narcissistic personality disorder with emotionally unstable, dissocial and anankastic traits[21] is still present.

However, due to his advanced age, a reduction of dangerousness had taken place: "There is no further persisting hypersexuality or sexual compulsion, and therefore there is no danger of him committing a sexually or non-sexually motivated violent offence again."

---

[21] *Anankastic or obsessive-compulsive personality disorder is characterised by a pronounced urge for order and perfection, as well as extreme striving for control.*

In addition, the expert emphasised that further therapy measures would no longer make sense, as Mr Josef F was only "superficially willing to undergo therapy" and there was no expectation of any change given his age.

Thereupon, the competent Regional Court Krems ordered the release of Josef F from the forensic detention. However, the public prosecutor's office did not agree and filed an appeal, arguing that Josef F's "serious and untreatable mental illness", caused by his incarceration, would "indisputably continue to exist". There would be no convincing indications that the danger had already been sufficiently reduced.

Josef F was given the opportunity to comment, and his response was surprising - he wanted to stay in the psychiatric detention! He argued that he was taking advantage of the many therapy options, which would not be possible in a regular prison. And: "Not least, another point that is important for me and my survival. In this section, I am in a protected area. In the past, I was already attacked twice outside the ward and beaten severely. If I were transferred to the regular prison, I would possibly be exposed to physical attacks again and I would not be able to survive. I would have to fear for life and limb, as I have hardly any possibility to defend myself due to my age. I therefore request that the appeal of the public prosecutor's office be upheld, the decision be overruled and that my continued stay in the psychiatric detention be ordered."

The Higher Regional Court Vienna subsequently upheld the appeal of the public prosecutor's office and determined the necessity of Josef F's continued placement in an institution for mentally abnormal offenders.

Meanwhile, Josef F has entrusted me to represent him under

criminal law. I will do everything in my power to have him released from the forensic placement. Certainly, he has committed despicable crimes that have caused a stir far beyond the borders of this country and have gone down in criminal history. Like many criminals, Josef F has carved out his own interpretation of the events. An interpretation that gradually solidified in his mind as the "truth".

No, he is not crazy. But his views are unshakable, and therapies will not be able to change that. At almost ninety, he is at an age when hardly anyone is able to gain new insights into life or break out of rigid attitudes.

On the other hand, however, the advanced age has likely led to a reduction of the sex drive. His former sexual promiscuity has long since given way to other interests, such as maintaining his own health or occupying himself with intellectual things, like reading and writing.

Josef F has become a quiet, now elderly prisoner, who may one day no longer be physically capable of handling everyday prison life. His fear of regular prison is understandable, but it does not justify keeping him in the forensic placement. As long as he is in prison, the state has the obligation to protect him.

I can already hear them shouting their phrases of how "a life-long sentence must stay life-long". Those who condemn my wanting to understand the darker sides of the human soul. To them, I like to say to their face: "Keep me from judging a person, before I've walked a mile in his moccasins"[22].

---

[22] *a proverb handed down by the Native Americans*

Manufactured by Amazon.ca
Acheson, AB